God's Little Book of Fire

GOD'S LITTLE BOOK OF FIRE by David Darbey

©2019 David Darbey, Abbotsford, BC All rights reserved.

BRV Publishing
First edition 2019

Scripture taken from the Revised standard version of the Holy
Bible are used under Fair Use guidelines from Ignatius Press.

Printed in Canada

ISBN 978-0-9812183-9-7

Cover and page layout by Brian Rodda.
www.brianrodda.ca

Table of Contents

Acknowledgements.

Thank you to my hidden jewel Jude who has always believed and always encouraged.

Thanks to Nick Teows for his valuable help with research and editing.

Thanks to Dave Rodda for his idea of turning these teachings into a book.

Thank you to Ross Roads Community Church for caring about people who are struggling, and for their help getting this book published.

And thanks to Brian Rodda for his patience and good suggestions.

GOD'S LITTLE BOOK OF FIRE

Spiritual and practical help for Christians fighting sexual addiction

Many Christians today live with some kind of sexual addiction. The following program was developed to assist and support those who are sincerely wanting to find a way out. The program provides 12 weeks of Bible based instruction and like other recovery programs employs a step by step method. The step by step approach is based on the understanding that addiction is a complex problem. Inside any addiction there are actually many negative habits interwoven and working together. Sexual addiction is like a thick rope made up of individual strands; there are not one but many habits that need to be addressed.

Each step in the program requires breaking a habit that has been an obstacle to recovery in the past. These are referred to as habit strands and they are severed one at a time. A few of these are behaviours but most are unhelpful and habitual ways of thinking. When *This program is open to all regardless of the type of sexual addiction. Mutual respect is required of group members and strict confidentiality is enforced.* all twelve habit strands are broken a much more resilient person emerges who is able to resist temptation when it arises. The ultimate goal is to change the addict rather than just the addiction.

To assist with understanding the nature of sexual addiction a metaphor has been employed. Each recovery step is compared to some aspect of a forest fire. This metaphor has been chosen because the Bible refers to sexual desire as being a lot like a fire. On the following page are listed the twelve steps of recovery with their corresponding habit strands. Included is a ranking system for wildfires employed by fire fighting crews.

	RECOVERY STEP	**HABIT STRAND**
	"Moving forward to"	*"Letting go of"*

1)	BEING INFORMED	IGNORANCE
2)	ADMITTING DEFEAT	DENIAL
3)	DRAWING NEAR	DISTANCE
4)	BELIEVING	DISCOURAGEMENT

5)	EXAMINING SIN	NAIVETY ABOUT SIN
6)	TAKING RESPONSIBILITY	EXCUSES
7)	CONFESSING	SECRECY
8)	REPENTING	COMPROMISE

9)	GIVING	SELFISHNESS
10)	MAKING AMENDS	EGOISM
11)	DEVELOPING DISCIPLINE	LAZINESS
12)	CONTROLING THE MIND	IMPURITY

. . . .

WILDFIRES

RANK 1   *smouldering ground fire*

RANK 2   *low vigor surface fire*

RANK 3   *running surface fire*

RANK 4   *vigorous surface fire*

RANK 5   *crown fire*

RANK 6   *conflagration*

STEP 1: Being Informed

Duff

As the seasons pass trees litter the forest floor with decaying plant matter. This collection of accumulated sticks, cones, needles, bark, and leaves is called "duff." The layer of debris can sometimes grow to two feet thick. During the long hot dry months of summer duff becomes bone dry and crackles underfoot. It is the ideal tinder material for wildfires. Half of forest fires start on the forest floor when a cigarette butt, or campfire ember lands on tinder dry duff. The more duff that has been allowed to accumulate, the greater the risk of a fire growing quickly out of control. In the same way debris accumulates in our minds over time and provides the perfect environment for the fires of addiction to ignite and grow. This mental duff is a collection of: misinformation, incorrect beliefs, assumptions, and uninformed opinions that render us naive about how sexual obsession works. The greater our unawareness of the truth, about how addiction takes hold, the greater risk we run of being caught up in it. People serious about fighting the fires of lust need to clear their minds of ignorance, and become better informed about the dangers of sexual compulsion.

"For a burning place has long been prepared."
— *Isa 30.33*

Letting Go of Ignornace

A major impediment to recovery is lack of knowledge. We avoid knowledge because we don't really want to know how trapped we are. In step one you will become more informed by examining: the addictive cycle, habits and the brain, levels of addiction, and sexual sins of the Bible. This information is difficult to face because it brings to light the strength of obsession that a sex addict is under, and reveals how much work it takes to recover. (Much of the information in this section has been taken from Patrick Carne's very helpful book, "Out of the Shadows.")

THE ADDICTIVE CYCLE
Sexually addictive behaviour follows a predictable cycle.

1) Preoccupation

The first step in the evolution of sexual misbehaviour happens in the mind. We think wrong before we do wrong.

* "For from within, out of the heart of man, come evil thoughts, fornication, theft, murder, adultery." Mk 7.21

At this point in the cycle an addict becomes preoccupied; his mind is engrossed and entertained with thoughts and fantasies of sex. This is the temptation phase.

2) Excitement

The second stage is the building up of excitement before the act. This is the planning stage with it's: watching, waiting, flirtation, preparation, and sometimes routines. This phase of heightened anticipation is mood altering. Hormones alter body functions and the addict becomes intoxicated with desire. For adrenaline junkies, elements of risk or danger will further fuel the lust they feel. For many this suspense stage is the most exhilarating and addictive part of the cycle. This is the "getting high" phase.

- "Each person is tempted when he is lured and enticed by his own desire." – Jam 1.14

3) Compulsion

This is the stage when the addict commits the sexual act that he's been fantasizing about. The addict feels strong compulsion that he is unable to control. Despite promises to themselves, God, and others, addicts are powerless to resist their urges. Paradoxically however, it is the very power of the compulsion that can present a door of hope. It is at this stage that an addict may be alarmed at his own powerlessness, and consider reaching out for help.

- "In my distress I called upon the Lord...He delivered me from my strong enemy, for they were too mighty for me. Ps 18.6&17

4) Despair

After giving in to his cravings the addict feels despair. This is caused by a sense of failure at not being able to keep his resolution, and by the loss of hope that he will ever be any different. He will likely feel shame, self loathing, depression, and may also feel self-pity. This sense of despair ironically only serves to fuel his lust, for it is his despair that will eventually causes him to seek out solace. Predictably he returns to the source of comfort that he has always counted on. The addict reignites his desire in order to get over feeling bad, and the cycle begins again. Once more around the endless circle he is pulled as he attempts to fill his unfillable void.

- "All streams run to the sea, but the sea is not full; to the place where the streams flow, there they flow again." Eccl 1.7

HABITS AND THE BRAIN

Our brain is full to the brim with millions and millions of neurons rapidly firing signals to tell your body what to do. At this moment thousands of neurons are firing and sending messages to other neurons, passing on important information. One of the ways the neurons in our brain help us is to enable us to form habits. Habits are efficient and spare us time and energy whenever we are engaged in repetitive behaviours. This is helpful for many good habits like riding a bike, but it poses a problem when we are faced with damaging habits. When we decide to create any new habit (good or bad), a circuit of neurons begins to form. Once a circuit is established a trigger neuron is capable of setting into motion a predictable reaction along the new neural pathway. This reaction becomes an automatic response that makes it easier for us to keep the new habit going. Unfortunately for sexual addicts this means that one simple trigger can set off a lust neuron circuit. One look at the wrong thing can engage a habit response and suddenly we are well down the road to the point of no return.

This is the reason sexual addiction is very difficult to beat. Through constant repetition we have formed a strong negative neural pathway. Our brain has become hardwired to automatically carry out our habitual behaviours. Once triggered, our neurons fire unerringly in just the way that we have trained them.

Addicts must face what they are up against. They are going to have to invest the time and effort it takes to change their brain in order to become free.

- Do not be conformed to this world but be transformed by the renewal of your mind. Rom 12.2

LEVELS OF ADDICTION

Psychologists have broken down the more common sexual addictions into 3 levels. These levels represent how society views the behaviours, whether there are any victims, and if legal sanctions are present.

10

Level One: masturbation, compulsive relationships, pornography, prostitution, and anonymous sex.

These behaviours are considered level one because in our culture they are thought of as more or less tolerable, they have few sanctions, and are perceived as victimless crimes. This does not however mean that level one compulsive behaviours do not create victims, or cause serious problems in a person's life.

Masturbation

• is a normal and healthy sexual activity, but compulsive masturbators lead a secret life. It can become an obsessive central part of every day.

Compulsive Relationships

• are when an addict makes their partner an obsession. This leaves the partner feeling that the relationship is contingent upon their sexual performance. They feel exploited and victimized by the addict's sexual needs.

Pornography

• is characterized by a desire for heightened sexual arousal in the absence of any relationship. After time the obsession can become more significant than being in any important relationship. (Considered much more serious if it is child porn.)

Prostitution

• is attractive to addicts because it is a quick fix that involves few entanglements, but it is expensive and often requires elaborate lies to explain the missing money.

Anonymous Sex

• is when people find sexual arousal through sex with strangers. For many, the more risky or dirty the encounter, the more exciting the sex. Such people find that they are unable to enjoy normal sex within healthy loving relationships.

Level Two: exhibitionism, voyeurism, indecent phone calls, indecent liberties, harassment

These behaviours create obvious victims, and offenders are dealt with through legal sanctions. Society however views such behaviours mainly as nuisance offences, and views the offenders more as pathetic than dangerous.

Exhibitionism
• is exposing oneself in public or on the internet.

Voyeurism
• is peering secretly into others' private lives in the hope of observing nudity or sexual activity. (Made much more prevalent through the internet)

Indecent phone calls
• is making phone calls in order to make suggestive statements, ask embarrassing questions, reveal inappropriate things, or make verbal assaults.

Indecent Liberties
• are inappropriate touches like purposely pressing into someone in a crowd, or "accidentally" brushing breasts and buttocks with the hand.

Harassment
• is using unwanted and inappropriate, suggestive, or lewd language. It can be coercive when coming from a boss or someone in authority.

Level Three: child molestation, child pornography, incest, rape

Level three behaviours show clear violations of another person, often the most vulnerable. Society shows little tolerance or compassion for offenders and legal sanctions are severe.

Child molestation
• involves any kind of sexual behaviour with children including: viewing pornography with them, voyeuristic behaviour, exposing, fondling, and sexual acts.

Child pornography
• is viewing, storing, and especially sharing sexualized images of children.

Incest
• is having sex with any aged family member, but sanctions are more severe when children are involved.

Rape
• is non consensual sex and includes rendering the victim defenceless through alcohol or date rape drugs. (It can also be present within a marriage.)

SEXUAL SINS OF THE BIBLE

Two things need to be noted at the outset of this subsection. Firstly, this world and God's people have very different standards regarding right and wrong. For the Christian our standards for sexual behaviour come from the scriptures. This does not mean that these are the standards we should use to judge people who are not part of the Body of Christ. We can only apply these teachings to those who strive to obey God, and have the Holy Spirit within them as their teacher.

• For what have I to do with judging outsiders? Is it not those inside the church whom you are to judge? God judges those outside. 1st Cor 5.12

Secondly, the high moral standards of scripture sometimes challenge our belief that the Bible is indeed God's word. (It says many things that we find hard to swallow.) We will need to come clear in our minds whether we do, or do not trust that the Bible accurately represents how God feels.

- All scripture is inspired by God and profitable for teaching, for reproof, for correction, and for training in righteousness. 2nd Tim 3.16

Described below are sexual behaviours that are not included in the previous list of common sexual addictions. These are sexual practices which are mostly not regarded as aberrant by our culture but according to scripture are harmful, full of obsession, and are displeasing to God. Engaging in these behaviours comes with consequences for Christians.

- "For it is time for judgement to begin with the household of God." 1st Pet 4.17

Fornication (sex out of wedlock)
- For this is the will of God, your sanctification: that you abstain from unchastity; that each of you know how to take a wife for himself in holiness and honour, not in the passion of lust like heathen who do not know God; that no man transgress, and wrong his brother in this matter, because the Lord is an avenger in all these things, as we solemnly forewarned you. 1st Thess 4.3-6

Seduction (Men and women are equally capable of seductive behaviour)
- With much seductive speech she persuades him; with her smooth talk she compels him. All at once he follows her... he does not know that it will cost him his life. Pr 7. 21&23
- Holding the form of religion but denying the power of it. Avoid such people. For among them are those who make their way into households and capture weak women. 2nd Tim 3.5-6

Lust of the eye (Includes pornography)
- "But I say to you everyone who looks at a woman lustfully has already committed adultery with her in his heart." Mt 5.28

Homosexuality

* For this reason God gave them up to dishonourable passions. Their women exchanged natural relations for unnatural, and the men likewise gave up natural relations with women and were consumed with passion for one another, men committing shameless acts with men and receiving in their own persons the due penalty for their error. Rom 1.26-27

Adultery

* Let marriage be held in honour among all, and let the marriage bed be undefiled; for God will judge the immoral and the adulterous. Heb 12.4

Sexual abuse within marriage

(It is not uncommon for partners to feel sexually coerced. This can happen through intimidation, pressure, belittling, bullying, pouting, or even quoting scripture, but whenever one is being treated in a way that they do not wish to be treated, it is abuse.)

* "Husbands love your wives and do not be harsh with (embitter) them." Col 3.19

NOTES

_____

_____

_____

_____

_____

_____

_____

_____

_____

STEP 2: Admitting Defeat

Smouldering Ground Fire

A smouldering ground fire has no visible flame and is barely spreading. It is a rank one fire (lowest on the wildfire scale.) A ground fire is actually an underground fire that is staying alive by consuming fuels within the soil like roots, decaying matter, or peat. Of no great hazard in itself, it does pose a serious threat if ignored. At any time it can burn through to the surface and cause a flare-up which can ignite the forest. If you are living with denial of your sexual addiction, you are only suppressing the problem and not extinguishing it. Given the right conditions it can resurface and cause damage and harm.

"Can a man carry fire in his bosom and his clothes not be burned?"

— Pr 6.27

Letting Go of Denial

SEXUAL IMMORALITY IS SERIOUS BUSINESS

If you have taken step one and are have decided to continue reading this, then you already know that aspects of your life are displeasing to God.

- But fornication and all impurity or greed must not even be named among you as is fitting among saints. Eph 5.3

16

You probably have also realized that you have behaviour that is harmful to your own spiritual development.

- Beloved I beseech you as aliens and exiles to abstain from the lusts of the flesh that wage war against your soul. 1st Pet 2.11

Also you may have come to see that your actions could harm others now or in the future, and that by yielding to temptation you could cause others to fall.

- Woe to the world for temptations to sin! For it is necessary that temptations come, but woe to the man by whom the temptation comes. Mt 18.7

DENIAL

Ever since the garden of Eden when man does something he is ashamed of, he hides. Adam and Eve hid from God behind a tree and we hide behind denial. Why do we do this? Why won't we readily admit our wrong? Is it because we feel embarrassed and ashamed? Is it because we think we will be rejected? Or is it because deep down we know that acknowledging our sin would be the first step in giving it up?

Addicts have a wide variety of ways of denying that there is a problem. They fabricate personal delusions so they won't have to admit the truth. Surely wherever there is sin, there is a lie close at hand. Perhaps you recognize some of your own lies of denial in the following list:

Minimizing -	It's no big deal
Making excuses -	I've been so stressed out lately
Blaming -	If she treated me right, I wouldn't have to resort to this
Predicting -	No one will ever find out
Ignoring -	I don't let myself think about it
Rationalizing -	The Bible is outdated in its view of sex
Postponing -	I will change, just not now
Helplessness -	I've tried to stop, I just can't help myself
Justification -	Cyber sex isn't with real people
Dismissing -	I'm not hurting anyone
Being affronted -	How dare you suggest such a thing about me?
Vowing -	It won't happen again

Christians have there own peculiar kinds of denial that can be especially misleading, but scripture refutes them all.

Avoiding responsibility- It's not me, its sin in me that's doing it. God doesn't expect me to be righteous while I still have my old nature.

* Do you not know that the unrighteous will not inherit the kingdom of God? Do not be deceived; neither the immoral, nor idolaters, nor adulterers, nor sexual perverts. 1st Cor 6.9

Claiming healing- God has delivered me from all my urges.

* Woe to the world for temptations to sin! For it is necessary that temptations come, but woe to the man by whom the temptation comes. Mt 18.7

Claiming unconditional grace- God accepts me the way I am.

* Unless your righteousness exceeds that of the scribes and the Pharisees, you will never enter the kingdom of heaven. Mt 5.20

Discounting Scripture- I'm only human, holiness is not really possible.

* But as he who called you is holy, be holy yourself in all your conduct; since it is written, "You shall be holy, for I am holy," 1st Per 1.15-16

Conforming- Every Christian I know has compromised their morals.

* Therefore I will judge you O house of Israel, each one according to his ways, says the Lord God. Ezek 18.30

Blaming the Devil- The devil takes control of me.

* Submit yourselves therefore to God, resist the devil and he will flee from you. Jam 4.7

THE NATURE OF ADDICTION

Getting past denial is absolutely necessary for change to occur. Admitting that we have an addiction, and that it has become unmanageable, is the first step toward taking responsibility for the problem. People who reach the point of seeking help have accepted a frightening fact, that they have lost control of themselves. They've tried many times in various ways to solve their problem and have failed. They don't want to be doing what they're doing, but when the urges come they are unable to control them. This is the biblical definition of addiction: being unable to stop doing what we don't want to do.

- I do not understand my own actions. For I do not do the thing I want, but I do the very thing I hate... For I know that nothing good dwells within me, that is in my flesh. I can will what is right but I cannot do it. For I do not do the good I want, but the evil I do not want is what I do. Rom 7.15 & 18-19

Those of you who have enrolled in this course have already struggled with denial. You've learned that wanting to change is not enough; that vowing to change is not enough; that praying about it is not enough. Perhaps you are finally willing to stop trying to beat this problem on your own. Being able to admit failure is a critical first step to recovery. It is only when we admit to ourselves that our problem is unmanageable that we will ever admit this to someone else, and seek help outside of ourselves.

- If we say we have no sin we deceive ourselves and the truth is not in us. If we confess our sins he is faithful and just to forgive our sins and cleanse us from all unrighteousness. 1st Jn 1. 8-9

So often in God's Kingdom things seem to work opposite to what we expect. God created the nation of Israel from Sarah who could no longer bear children. He chose David, a young boy with no military experience, to defeat Israel's most fearsome enemy - Goliath. He chose Paul, a violent man, to carry his message of love. Jesus suffered humiliation and death in order to free us from humiliation and death. Perhaps we should not be surprised then that overcoming addiction begins with admitting that we are overcome by addiction.

COURAGE

The first step to victory is defeat
The first step to success is failure
The first step to becoming strong is being weak
The first step to wholeness is need
The first step to dignity is humility

People suffer for years in secret defeat knowing the damage their habit is doing to their walk with God. They wonder why they can't beat their sexual addiction. The answer is simple, they haven't gotten help. You can't beat sexual addiction on your own! It's time to let go of the mistaken notion that you should be able to solve this problem. It's time to expose your shameful secret. Only if you are willing to humble yourself, admit your defeat and confess your need, will the door to freedom be opened for you. Only then can our great Saviour do the saving. He will send people to support you; people who have won their own battles with addiction and shame. Sexual addiction can be beaten through the body of Christ. We were never meant to carry these burdens all alone.

- Brethren, if a man is overtaken in any trespass, you who are spiritual should restore him in a spirit of gentleness. Look to yourselves lest you too be tempted. Bear one another's burdens and so fulfil the law of Christ. Gal 6.1-2

List any people in your circle of acquaintances "Who are spiritual" that you think might be willing to assist you in your recovery. This could be through: praying, listening, keeping you accountable, being there when you face temptation, or just by joining in healthy activities with you.

_____

_____

_____

_____

_____

_____

_____

_____

_____

STEP 3: Drawing Near

Drought

This manual was completed in the summer of 2015 in the midst of an unprecedented drought. The west coast of B.C. (often called the wet coast) historically has mild summers punctuated with frequent periods of rain. This year there hasn't been any significant rainfall since the beginning of May. Temperatures have been well above average. To make things worse last winter was very dry which left a very low snow pack, so this summer the streams are barely running. A walk in the woods reveals crispy ferns and dry yellow leaves littering the forest floor. The deciduous trees are shedding their leaves prematurely in a desperate attempt to survive the drought. These are perfect conditions for wildfires, and the risk of forest fires most days this summer has been rated at extreme. If you are in a place where God seems distant and your prayers are seldom answered; if the Bible seems dry and lifeless and you are lukewarm about obedience; then you are in a spiritual drought. These are the perfect conditions in which sexual addiction can flare up and grow out of control. To fight fire you must have water; you must find the source of living water to have any hope of overcoming your addiction.

"It is the time to seek the Lord, that he may come and rain salvation upon you."
— Hos 10.1

I'M READY

Lord, I'm sick of myself
I'm sick of my sin
I'm ready to change
and get down to work

I have been hardened
and indifferent to your voice
I know I have to seek you
and open up my heart to you

I'm ready to care about you again, and how you feel

When we have a sexual addiction our relationship with God is compromised. This is characterized by a sense of distance rather than intimate fellowship.

- If we say we have fellowship with him while we walk in darkness, we lie and do not live according to the truth. 1st Jn 1.6

This distance settles in because our addiction has caused us to relinquish a large part of our will to what the Bible calls, "The flesh." This word refers not to our bodies, but to the self-serving nature that abides in all of us.

- For I know that nothing good dwells within me, that is in my flesh. I can will what is right, but I cannot do it. Rom 7.18

This unfortunate part of us has no interest in being close to God. In fact it is in direct opposition to God .

- For the mind that is set on the flesh is hostile to God; it does not submit to God's law, indeed it cannot. Rom 8.7

When our flesh is in charge of our lives our spirits suffer. Our prayer life withers and we isolate ourselves from truly spiritual people who may challenge us. The scriptures no longer feel alive, and our thirst for God fades. Our experience of God's presence becomes rare, and we don't hear him speaking to us personally anymore. We grow out of touch with God and ironically wonder where he has wandered off to. The more satiated our flesh is, the more emaciated our spirits become. If we are living for our flesh we are dying spiritually.

UNDESIRABLE QUALITIES OF THE FLESH

1. It serves sin rather than God:

I serve the law of God with my mind but with my flesh I serve the law of sin. Rom 7.25

2. It tends toward sexual sin:

The works of the flesh are plain: fornication impurity, licentiousness Gal 5.19

3. It stunts our spiritual growth:

I, brethren, could not address you as spiritual men, but as men of the flesh, as babes in Christ. I fed you with milk, not solid food; for you were not ready for it; and even yet you are not ready, for you are still of the flesh. 1st Cor 3.1-3

4. It is weak:

Watch and pray that you may not enter into temptation; the spirit is willing but the flesh is weak. Mt 26.41

5. It displeases God:

Those who are in the flesh cannot please God. Rom 8.8

As long as you are living in "your flesh" you will have great difficulty breaking your addiction. In a fleshy state you habitually serve yourself, and are dominated by your old selfish nature. Your flesh doesn't want to do anything difficult or demanding. Like water, it will always seek the path of least resistance.

- The gate is wide and the way is easy that leads to destruction, and those who enter by it are many. Mt 7.13

Trying to change your self, while being distant from God and living for the flesh, is like trying to make water flow uphill. Without fail, it will eventually find a way to head back downhill. The flesh is too weak to stand up to the flesh. To beat addiction you must become spiritually strong.

HOW DO I FIND SPIRITUAL STRENGTH?

1) CHOOSE YOUR MASTER

We need to come to the realization that in this life we are all slaves, but we do have a choice who we are slaves of, either our own fleshy nature, or God.

- Do you not know that if you yield yourselves to anyone as obedient slaves, you are slaves of the one whom you obey, either of sin, which leads to death, or of obedience that leads to righteousness. Rom 6.16

There is an escape from being enslaved to the flesh, but there is a price to pay. We must completely give up living for ourselves. This for many, is unpalatable. They want Jesus to help with one area of their lives that is out of control, but they aren't willing to hand over their whole life to him. Yet Jesus has made it plain that he wants to be not just saviour, but Lord. We are mistaken if we think he would set us free from addiction while we are still choosing to live for ourselves. As long as we prefer our flesh over him, we are choosing to be spiritual weaklings.

- To set the mind on the flesh is {spiritual} death, but to set the mind on the Spirit is {spiritual} life and peace. Rom 8.6

Making Jesus Christ your master is a drastic decision. It is surrendering the control of your life to Christ. It is telling him from the heart that for the rest of your time on earth you are no longer going to live for what you want. You are changing your mind, and are committing yourself to live for Jesus and what he wants.

- And he died for all, that those who live may no longer live for themselves, but for him who for their sake died and was raised. 2nd Cor 5.15

This must be an all-encompassing decision with no holding back. Relationships, finances, plans, health, entertainment & recreation etc. must all be given to him. He wants to be Lord of your whole life. You can't select some areas of your life where you will serve God, and others where you serve the flesh. It doesn't work.

- No one can serve two masters; for he will either hate the one and love the other, or he will be devoted to the one and despise the other. Mt 6.24

Jesus wants our all. We are to love God with all our hearts, minds, souls, and strength because he loves us with all his heart, mind, soul, and strength. His commitment to us is not half-way, it is all the way. He expects the same kind of commitment in return.

- Indeed I count everything as loss for the surpassing worth of knowing Christ Jesus my Lord. For his sake I have suffered the loss of all things and count them as refuse, in order that I may gain Christ. Phil 3.8

2) DRAW NEAR TO YOUR MASTER

It is not enough to recommit your life to serving Christ. This dedication will fade unless you also recommit to your relationship with him. The power to change chronic addiction is a spiritual power. To receive this power you must repair the distance that has come between you and your Lord by making your relationship with Jesus Christ the most important thing in your life. Commit to spending at least an hour of quality time alone with him each day. If reconnecting with him is really your top priority, above anything else, then is spending an hour a day with him too much to ask?   Open up your heart to him; be honest and share with him everything on your mind. Return to the study of scripture, the Holy Spirit communicates through God's word of truth. This is how he comforts, instructs, and strengthens us. This is how he exposes lies in our minds and sets us free. The word of God made alive by the Spirit is the pure power that you need.

- For the word of God is living and full of power, sharper than any two edged sword, piercing to the division of soul and spirit, of joints and marrow, and discerning the thoughts and intentions of the heart. Heb 4.12

Filling yourself with truth is devastating to the flesh but it is refreshing and nourishing to your spirit. Spending time together with God and exploring his word will strengthen you spiritually. Your spirit will start asserting itself and standing up to your flesh, and you will gradually begin to regain your self control.

- If you continue in my word, you are truly my disciples, and you will know the truth and the truth will make you free. Jn 8.31-32

Concentrating our focus only on stopping an addiction is a mistake. This isn't really about stopping something, it is about starting something. If we manage to stop certain behaviours, without renewing our relationship with God, the change will not last. We will fall back under the dark dominion of our fleshy nature. To beat addiction we must change ourselves. We must become someone who can resist temptation. This happens through acquiring spiritual strength, strength that comes from being close to God.

- Submit yourselves therefore to God. Resist the devil and he will flee from you. Draw near to God and he will draw near to you. Jam 4.7-8

NOTES

_____

_____

_____

_____

_____

_____

_____

_____

_____

STEP 4: Choose To Believe

Spot Fires

Wildfires are frightening to behold. They can surge forward at 50km/hr when winds are strong. Rank 5 & 6 fires display a variety of what are termed "extreme fire behaviours." One of these behaviours is called spotting. When a fire is raging it develops its own strong updrafts due to tremendous heat soaring upwards. These thermal winds can carry embers thousands of feet into the air. Strong surface winds transport these embers up to 1.5 kilometres ahead of the advancing fire. Wherever they land they start new fires, and from these small spot fires new major fires spring up. In the same way out of control sexual behaviour throws out its

> ""Behold all you who kindle a fire, who set brands alight!"
>
> —Isa 50.11

embers. Their names are discouragement and despair. As mentioned previously in the section on the addiction cycle, the result of an addict giving into his urges is a welling up of despair. It is from these bouts of discouragement that the next flare up of compulsive behaviour will come. In a very real sense, through his sense of defeat, an addict rekindles his own fires. Finding a way to control discouragement will help to break this cycle.

Let Go Of Discouragement

Whenever we have a chronic area of defeat in our lives we become discouraged. Our minds fill up with damaging and negative "self talk." This can make us feel down on ourselves and spiritually depressed. Dealing with discouragement is a very important part of healing. Our battle for recovery is really a battle for our own mind. The critical voices in our head, particularly after we have had a fall, are always out to hurt us. They contain a toxic mix of other people's views of us, the devil's accusations, and our own low opinion of ourselves. The one voice that is on our side gets drowned out by all the negative criticism.

God does not criticize, accuse, or browbeat his children. If you are his child then you have his Spirit dwelling inside you. His Spirit is a counsellor, not a critic. The word Jesus used to describe the Holy Spirit is, "Parakletos." It means advocate, intercessor, or comforter. He is someone who isn't against you but is for you; someone who is on your side to assist you and gently guide you into the truth.

- And I will pray the Father and he will give you another counsellor, to be with you forever, even the Spirit of truth. Jn 14.16

This does not mean that God never corrects us. The Holy Spirit does convict us of sin but it is done out of love and is never meant to discourage.

- Those whom I love I reprove and chasten, so be zealous and repent. Rev 3.19

28

CRITICISM / CONVICTION

Discourages us from trying	Creates motivation to change
Increases confusion	Brings clear revelation
Is repetitive & nagging	Is spoken once
Is harmful	May hurt, but is helpful
Creates distance with God	Brings us closer to God
Makes us hard on ourselves	Comes with forgiveness
Damages confidence	Improves confidence
Is harsh	Is gentle and peaceful
Causes feelings of guilt & shame	Causes genuine remorse

We however, have difficulty distinguishing God's loving voice of conviction from the harsh inner voices of criticism. How do we learn to sort out the Spirit's voice?

To help us become free from discouragement {which only feeds addiction} we need to challenge what we believe about ourselves. We need to arrive at a more positive and resilient belief based on how God sees us. We need answers to three essential questions.

1) DOES JESUS LOVE ME AND WANT TO HELP ME?
2) DOES HE FORGIVE ME?
3) IS HE ABLE TO FREE ME FROM MY ADDICTION?

1) Does Jesus love me and want to help me?

Jesus described himself as a doctor, whose mission it was to welcome and treat those who were sick with sin.

- Those who are well have no need of a physician, but those who are sick; I have not come to call the righteous, but sinners to repentance. Lk 5.31-32
- The Lord builds up Jerusalem; he gathers the outcasts of Israel. He heals the broken hearted and binds up their wounds. Ps 147.2-3

Jesus Christ has a heart of healing. No one who sincerely seeks his help will ever be turned away. If we are willing to repent it doesn't matter to him what sins we have committed. It is his great desire to heal, and he desires to heal you.

- The sacrifice acceptable to God is a broken spirit; a broken and contrite heart, O God, thou will not despise. Ps 51.17

The whole reason that Jesus went to the cross was on behalf of sinful people. Jesus died for people just like you and me. He is absolutely full of compassion for sinners and has proven it.

- While we were still weak, at the right time Christ died for the ungodly. Why, one would hardly die for a righteous man - though perhaps for a good man one would even dare to die. But God shows his love for us in that while we were yet sinners Christ died for us. Rom 5.6-8

2) *Does he forgive me?*

On the cross Jesus accomplished some very mysterious things. If you have welcomed him as your saviour then you are the beneficiary of an extraordinary miracle. Jesus has already, once and for all, traded places with you in the heavenly places. The theological term for this transaction is "substitution." This means he has taken upon himself everything about you that displeases God. He took ownership and responsibility for your sin as if it were his own. Up upon the cross Jesus took the blame for all your sin, including your sexual addiction.

- The Lord has laid on him the iniquity of us all. Isa 53.6
- Christ redeemed us from the curse of the law, having become a curse for us. Gal 3.13
- For our sake he made him to be sin who knew no sin, so that in him we might become the righteousness of God. 2nd Cor 5.21

Because he took the blame for you he also took upon himself the punishment that you deserved. Jesus suffered for you to save you from suffering.

- He was wounded for our transgressions, he was bruised for our iniquities; upon him was the chastisement that made us whole, and with his stripes we are healed. Isa 53.5

Even with all this Jesus' gift of grace to you was not complete. In trading places with you he had something even more mysterious in mind. Not only did he want to take your sin, but he wanted to give you his righteousness in exchange. The righteousness you couldn't achieve in a thousand life times, is his free gift to you.

- If, because of one man's trespass, death reigned through that one man, much more will those that receive the abundance of grace and the free gift of righteousness reign in life through the one man Jesus Christ. Rom 5.17
- And you, who were once estranged and hostile in mind, doing evil deeds, he has now reconciled in his body of flesh by his death, in order to present you holy and blameless and irreproachable before him. Col 1.21-22

This is why he is able to forgive you, because he has already forgiven you. The punishment you deserve has already been meted out, and he has put his own robe of righteousness around your shoulders. Now and forever God sees you as forgiven and blameless in Christ.

- I will greatly rejoice in the Lord, my soul shall exalt in my God; for he has clothed me with the garments of salvation, he has covered me with the robe of righteousness. Isa 61.10

3) Is he able to free me from my addiction?

The pull of addiction is very strong. It's hard for people not living with it to understand. At full strength the impulses seem impossible to withstand. Those who suffer with it know that it feels like being trapped in a boxing ring with an opponent twice your size. It feels like you are doomed to be eternally at the mercy of this foe. But this is a fight you can win because you do not have to stand in that ring alone. Jesus Christ is a fearsome warrior who set out from heaven in order to fight on your behalf. His mission was to destroy satan and free us from bondage.

- The Spirit of the Lord God is upon me, because the Lord has anointed me to bring good tidings to the afflicted; he has sent me to bind up the broken hearted, to proclaim liberty to the captives, and the opening of the prison to those who are bound. Isa 61.1
- The reason the Son of God appeared was to destroy the work of the devil. 1st Jn 3.8

Jesus' work upon the cross has made the impossible possible. Something happened there to strip away sin's power and open up a way for us to be free of it. His sacrifice made a way for us to be free not only from the penalty of sin, but also from its power.

- But now that you have been set free from sin and have become slaves of God, the return you get is sanctification, and its end, eternal life. Rom 6.22
- For sin will have no dominion over you since you are no longer under law but under grace. Rom 6.14

For someone struggling with sexual addiction this is something difficult to believe. How is it that sin has no dominion over me? In the book of Romans Paul explains a mystery. Jesus wasn't the only one to die that day.

- We know that our old self was crucified with him so that the sinful body {our fleshy nature} might be destroyed, and we might no longer be enslaved to sin. Rom 6. 6
- I have been crucified with Christ; it is no longer I who live, but Christ who lives in me. Gal 2.20
- Those who belong to Christ Jesus have crucified the flesh with its passions and desires. Gal 5.24

If you are willing to accept it, your old fleshy self is already dead and defeated and you do not have to obey it anymore. There is a real alternative and it is to yield to Christ and walk in his Spirit. This is a supernatural life, hidden to those still living in the flesh, but revealed to all who completely surrender to Jesus.

- The unspiritual man does not receive the things of the Spirit of God, for they are a folly to him, and he is not able to understand them because they are spiritually discerned. 1st Cor 2.14

In truth you are actually a new spiritual being. You aren't your old self anymore at all. In your inner self you are a spirit. Have you discovered yet your true self?

- From now on we regard no one from a human point of view… If anyone is in Christ he is a new creation; the old has passed away, behold the new has come. 2nd Cor 5.16-17

This is the spiritual solution to addiction. This is how Jesus can empower you to change. You can receive power and guidance beyond your own strength. By living in the Spirit you can to stand up to any and all demands of the flesh.

- If you live according to the flesh you will die, but if by the Spirit you put to death the deeds of the body you will live. Rom 8.13
- That according to the riches of his glory he may grant you to be strengthened with might through his Spirit in the inner man. Eph 3.16
- In all these things we are more than conquerors through him who loved us. Rom 8.37

It is such a freeing realization when we understand that we get to choose what we believe about ourselves. We can keep believing our old discouraging self-talk, or choose to believe what God says about us. You can choose to adopt a new set of beliefs about yourself, based on what Jesus has accomplished on your behalf. God has already demonstrated his love for you. Why wouldn't he help you now?

- He who did not spare his own son, but gave him up for us all, will he not also give us all things with him? Rom 8.32

Transform your belief about yourself, and you will transform your life.

A NEW CREED

I believe Jesus is for me and not against me
I believe Jesus is my physician and wants to make me well
I believe Jesus died for people just like me
I believe Jesus traded places with me on the cross
I believe Jesus has already been punished for my sins
I believe Jesus has forgiven me once and for all
I believe Jesus has given me his own righteousness
I believe Jesus fights for me
I believe Jesus has already defeated my fleshy nature
I believe Jesus has made me a brand new spiritual being
I believe Jesus, by his Spirit, is able to free me from my addiction
I believe Jesus Christ loves me more than anyone ever will

Meditation Verses:

2nd Pet 1.3, Jn 16.13, Jn 8.31-32, Rom 6.17-18, 2nd Tim 1.7, Heb 2.17, Heb 10.14, Rom 8.33, Gal 5.1

NOTES

Step 5: Examine Sin

Creeping Surface Fire

A creeping surface fire is classified as rank 1 and is the most common form of forest fire. It spreads slowly over the ground consuming grass, shrubs, and duff. The flames are low and of all the types of wildfires, the creeping surface fire appears to be the most manageable. Typically seen by fire fighters as a low priority these fires are, (depending on the location) sometimes allowed to burn themselves out. Fire crews know however that they run a risk by permitting the fire to keep burning. They are gambling that conditions won't change. If they are wrong, what seems harmless at present could flare up and cause serious harm in the future. In the same way Christians put up with what they see as low level sexual sin in their lives. This might include: lusting with the eyes, pornography with masturbation, adulterous fantasies, flirtation/seduction, sexual coercion within marriage, etc. Such behaviours are unfortunately quite common amongst Christians and it is because of their commonness that they are not treated with more alarm. This attitude displays an ignorance about how sin works. When we permit sexual sin any place in our lives it will always seek an opportunity to grow stronger. A stressful pe-

"How great a forest is set ablaze by a small fire"
—Jam 3.5

riod, a relationship problem, an unexpected temptation, can all provide the right conditions for a creeping sin fire to turn into an all out conflagration. This is why Paul warned the Corinthian church not to tolerate sexual sin in their midst; "A little leaven leavens the whole lump." 1st Cor 5. To be spiritually safe these small fires must be extinguished, otherwise it is only a question of time before they flare up and cause real harm.

Let Go Of Naivety About Sin

This world may call sexual addiction an illness, but the Bible clearly calls it sin. In Bible terms any addiction is sin. Addiction just means we have allowed an area of the flesh to gain control of us. When we succumb to wrong sexual behaviour we are displeasing God and our relationship with him will be affected. Sin always puts distance between us and the Lord.

- Behold, the Lord's hand is not shortened, that it cannot save, or his ears dull that it cannot hear; but your iniquities have made a separation between you and your God. Isa 59.1-2

THE ANATOMY OF SIN

Understanding the anatomy of sin and how it gets a hold of us, is integral to overcoming it. There are actually varying levels of sin which God deals with in different ways. A useful definition of sin is, "anything that displeases God." In the book of James there is an illuminating passage that explains the growth of sin. James describes sin as having four developmental stages similar to the development of the human fetus.

- Each person is tempted when he is lured and enticed by his own desire. Then desire, when it has conceived, gives birth to sin; and sin when it is full grown brings forth death. Jam 1.14-15

DESIRE – YOUNG SIN – FULL GROWN SIN – DEATH

STAGE 1: DESIRE

We all are tempted and lured by desire, and this is where all sin begins. We don't sin without first wanting to. Even Jesus was tempted by desire.

- For we have not a high priest who is unable to sympathize with our weaknesses, but one who in every respect has been tempted as we are, yet without sin. Heb 4.15

Even though desire gives birth to sin, it is not yet sin in itself. Jesus felt desire and temptation but wouldn't permit them to take root in his mind. Think of desire like a fertile egg. It has all the potential to create a new life but if it is not inseminated it will eventually die. This is by far the easiest time to deal with sin, when it is only a temptation. If however we entertain our desires and provide the right environment in our thought life, then sin will be conceived. It latches on and begins a period of gestation in our minds; and not content to remain only an embryo of our imagination, it strives to enter the realm of our behaviour. If we have not aborted desire then we have created sin, ready to be born into our world.

STAGE 2: YOUNG SIN

This is sin in its early stages. It is like an infant. It has not reached its full strength or developed a mind of its own. It is dependant upon us to feed it. These sins are in everyone's life. These are the unintentional stumbles and mistakes we all make. They are the occasional moments of weakness we all succumb to. Even righteous people lose their balance and fall sometimes.

- For a righteous man falls seven times, and rises again. Pr 24.16

God deals with this kind of sin by simply pointing it out or perhaps warning us. Discipline is not normally required.

- For the commandment is a lamp and the teaching is a light, and the reproofs of discipline are the way of life. Pr 6.23

Young sin is relatively easy to recover from. We may get a bruise or two when we stumble but we get up, brush ourselves off, and walk on. We are willing to repent, we learn our lesson, and we avoid going down that wrong path again.

We always have a choice what we do with our sin babies. We can euthanize them, or nurture them. We are deceiving ourselves if we think young sins are harmless. They always want to grow in size and strength. Ask any person the history of their sexual addiction, and they'll tell you that their problem began with relatively minor stumbles.

STAGE 3: FULL GROWN SIN

When young sin goes unchecked it doesn't diminish, it grows up. Its aim is to become strong enough to gain control. It ultimately wants to enslave you and force you to serve it.

- If you do not do well, sin is couching at the door; its desire is for you, but you must master it. Gen 4.7

Full-grown sin is strong and persistent. We can no longer call it just an occasional stumble. It has become deliberate and habitual. The person in this stage of sin is still fighting with temptation, but they are losing. They have made many attempts to repent, but are not able to stick to it. To God this kind of sin is more serious than young sin and requires discipline.

- Whoever knows what is right to do and fails to do it, for him it is sin. Jam 4.17
- And that servant who knew his master's will, but did not make ready or act according to that will, shall receive a severe beating. But he who did not know, and did what deserved a beating, shall receive a light beating. Lk 12.47-48

All sin has consequence, but deliberate sin has more severe consequence. God is our Father, and his love for us goes beyond just compassion. He shows another dimension of his love by caring enough to discipline us. If your sin has become full-grown then you have already been disregarding God's voice for quite a while. You've already shown that his warnings were not enough for you to change, so he must move on to some kind of action. If you have full grown sin in your life you won't get away with it. If you are honest, you can already see areas where his judgments are at work.

- Besides this, we have had earthly fathers to discipline us and we respected them. Shall we not much more be subject to the Father of spirits and live? For they disciplined us for a short time at their pleasure, but he disciplines us for our good, that we may share his holiness. Heb 12.9-10

Even though God may not be pleased with us, he still loves us. Even though we have allowed sin to grow to the point where it requires discipline, there is still bright hope. People in this stage do recognize that what they are doing is wrong, and they still want to change. They suffer bouts of Godly sorrow; it still matters to them what their Lord thinks of them. This ability to still feel sorry means they are still open to God, open to the sharp word of truth and open to discipline. The fact that you are in this program shows that you are calling out to God, and your heart is still turned toward your Father.

- For godly grief produces a repentance that leads to salvation and brings no regret. 2nd Cor 7.10

STAGE 4: DEATH

If we ignore God's voice and permit young sin to take hold, and then go on to ignore his discipline and permit full grown sin to continue, we then enter the last stage of sin. This is where full grown sin settles in and becomes our master. We are completely surrendered to it and powerless to disobey. At this point sin's aim is to destroy us spiritually and cause us to fall away from the Lord.

- For if, after they have escaped the defilements of the world through the knowledge of our Lord and saviour Jesus Christ, they are again entangled in them and overpowered, the last state has become worse for them than the first. 2nd Pet 2.20

This deadly stage of sin has a hardening effect upon our hearts. We start to lose the desire to repent, we no longer hope for change. We stop feeling sorry for our actions; in fact we start justifying them. We grow cold toward God, lose contact with him and turn our hearts away.

- Take care brethren lest there be in any of you an evil and unbelieving heart, leading you to fall away from the living God. But exhort one another every day, as long as it is called today,

39

that none of you may be hardened by the deceitfulness of sin. Heb 3.12-13

The truth is that Jesus' work on the cross is of no avail for those no longer willing to repent. Where there is no repentance there can be no forgiveness.

- For if we sin deliberately after receiving the knowledge of the truth, there no longer remains a sacrifice for sins, but a fearful prospect of judgment, and a fury of fire which will consume the adversaries. Heb 10.26-27

Those who refuse to acknowledge their sin and refuse to repent are the one group that Jesus can't help. If we stubbornly remain in this unrepentant state, then sin has achieved its original goal. Remember that our flesh is in direct opposition to God; your spiritual decline and demise has always been its intention.

- For the desires of the flesh are opposed to the Spirit. Gal 5.17
- Do not be deceived; God is not mocked, for whatever a man sows, that he will also reap. He who sows to his own flesh will from the flesh reap corruption. Gal 6.7

Thankfully even when we are completely given over to sin, God does not give up. He keeps trying to get our attention even when he's being deliberately ignored. A testament to his patience and persistence is that there are still some who do get rescued, from even the last stage of sin.

- My brethren, if anyone among you wanders from the truth and someone brings him back, let him know that whoever brings back a sinner from the error of his way will save his soul from death and cover a multitude of sins. Jam 5.19-20
- Convince some who doubt; save some, by snatching them out of the fire; on some have mercy with fear, hating even the garment spotted by the flesh. Jude 22-23

The definition of naivety is to be simple and unsuspecting. Having a naïve attitude toward sin can cost you everything. Sin is a powerful enemy capable of killing your soul. Its goal is to control you and eventually destroy you. The more naïve you are about its intentions, the more complacent you will be about its presence in your life.

- For the simple are killed by their turning away, and the complacence of fools destroys them. Pr 1.32

As a Christian with a any kind of sexual addiction you are in very real spiritual danger. You need to open your eyes, take seriously the peril you are in, and fight to win back control of your behaviour and your thought life.

NOTES

_____

_____

_____

_____

_____

_____

_____

_____

_____

_____

_____

_____

_____

_____

_____

_____

_____

_____

Step 6: Take Responsibility

Running Surface Fire

A running surface fire is a rank 3 or 4 fire that is rapidly moving. This fire has a well defined "head" with billowing gray-black smoke. It is starting to exhibit volatile fire behaviours like short range spotting, and candling. Candling is when single trees suddenly burst into flame from intense heat. Unlike the creeping surface fire the running fire is one that is starting to get out of control. This usually happens as a result of intensifying winds.

When someone is in the early stages of sexual sin they are often remorseful and repentant. In their early stages sin fires are slow moving with small flames, and can be relatively easily extinguished. But our sin fires grow in strength when they are fanned by the winds of our own excuses. Excuses are just lies that we tell ourselves to avoid the discomfort of feeling guilty. Sin thrives on such

"Exhort one another every day, as long as it is called, 'today,' that none of you be hardened by the deceitfulness of sin."

—Heb 3.13

dishonesty, and as we lie to ourselves a kind of deadening of our conscience takes place. Our behaviour no longer feels "as wrong" as it did at first. We are now not resisting sin but justifying it. Scripture refers to this as hardening of the heart. It is always associated with sin that is growing out of control.

Letting Go of Excuses

The more we lie to ourselves the more we believe the lie. This enables us to keep on sinning and provides the perfect conditions for the fire to spread.

- This is the way of an adulteress: she eats, and wipes her mouth and says, "I have done no wrong." Pr 30.20
- Their lies have led them astray...so I will send a fire upon Judah and it shall devour the strongholds of Jerusalem. Amos 2.4-5

It seems that it is human nature to avoid facing up to our mistakes. We often make excuses or blame others rather than take responsibility for our actions. Even in the garden of Eden, as far back as we can go in the Bible, we see a familiar scenario being acted out.

- And they heard the sound of the Lord walking in the garden in the cool of the day, and the man and his wife hid themselves from the presence of the Lord God among the trees of the garden. But the Lord called out to the man, and said to him, "Where are you?" And he said, "I heard the sound of thee in the garden and I was afraid, because I was naked; and I hid myself." He said, "Who told you that you were naked? Have you eaten of the tree which I commanded you not to eat?" The man said, "The woman who thou gavest to be with me, she gave me the fruit of the tree, and I ate." Then the Lord God said to the woman, "What is this that you have done?" The woman said, "The serpent beguiled me and I ate." Gen 3.8-13

Here is a sad but true allegory of our sin and how we all struggle to cover it up.

1) HIDING

"They hid themselves from the presence of the Lord."

Our first reaction after we sin is to try to hide it. We don't want to admit our failure to God or others, so we conceal it and sneak behind trees. Instead of being out in the open and going directly to God acknowledging what we've done, we choose to avoid him. It's not our sin in itself that causes this but our unwillingness to confess it. God hasn't gone anywhere, his presence is still there in the garden it is we who have moved away. He is forced into a mission of spiritual search and rescue calling out, "Where are you?"

2) FEAR
"I heard the sound of thee in the garden and I was afraid."

Any state of denial is the result of fear. Adam and Eve hid because they were afraid. Having chosen to conceal what they had done they were now afraid of exposure. This kind of guilty fear (as opposed to godly fear) is relationship destroying. You can't love someone you are afraid of. Adam and Eve didn't want to be close to God anymore. They preferred to keep him at a manageable distance. This is what fear of discovery does, it robs us of our intimacy with God and keeps him at arm's length. This is one of the reasons God hates sin.

3) LYING
"Because I was naked, I hid myself."

Where there is sin there is always a lie close at hand. Adam was in fact not naked when God was looking for him. He and Eve had first sewn aprons of fig leaves to cover themselves (which must have taken some time), and then they ran to hide from God. Adam did not hide because he was naked. He was just not willing to tell God the truth about what he'd done and so he told the first lie. We have since become masters at using lies to cover up the truth.
- The heart is deceitful above all things and desperately corrupt; who can understand it? Jer 17.9

4) BLAMING
"The woman that thou gavest to be with me, she gave me fruit of the tree, and I ate."

When directly confronted by God Adam starts to squirm. He

realizes he can't lie his way out of this and so he admits what he did. But this is no remorseful confession of wrong or taking responsibility. He's trying to avoid any consequences for his actions by blaming someone else. "Yes I did it, but it's not my fault!" he says. Notice the subtle way his answer to God is worded. He points out to God that the real culprit was someone God himself had brought into his life. Adam is shifting blame on to Eve as well as onto God. This illustrates how strong self-preservation is in us. Adam is willing to besmirch the only two he loves, in order to protect himself.

5) EXCUSES

"The serpent beguiled me, and I ate."

Eve also is not willing to take responsibility for what she has done. She claims she was tricked into disobeying so it wasn't her fault. The thing we so often forget about God is that he can see into our hearts and read our true motivations. Eve was living in paradise with access to all its bounty save one tree. Yet she was not content. She wanted something more. If selfish desire and discontent had not already been inside Eve then the devil would never have been able to tempt her. If she had loved God she would have run straight to her Father and told him of an evil presence in his garden. Yet she didn't, and "Why not?" is the question. There she was negotiating with God's sworn enemy because she was filled with craving. We can come up with a thousand excuses for why we sin but there is only one honest reason why; we want to. Our desire to please ourselves is stronger than our desire to please God.

Choosing the path of recovery over the path of addiction means taking a good hard look at the truth. We have to admit who really is to blame for our problem. The uncomfortable truth is that we are all responsible, through our choices, for the kind of life we are experiencing. As God has so often warned us, we reap exactly what we sow. Adam and Eve sowed dishonesty, concealment, denial, blaming, and excuses. They reaped pain, servitude, toil, difficulty, and expulsion from the garden. This however does not have to be our destiny. We can sow seeds of change.

SEEDS OF ACKNOWLEDGEMENT

Admit to God exactly what it is you have done wrong. Acknowledge how your choices have been self-serving. Tell him how inconsiderate you have been toward him. Search your heart and admit that your sin has harmed others, people that he cares about and died for. Acknowledge that you have been fraternizing with his enemies; that you have been cooperating with them to advance their cause against him. Come out of hiding and take responsibility for what your sin has done.

SEEDS OF RECONCILIATION

Adam and Eve permitted sin to come between them and their Father. They became afraid to get close to him, and enter his presence. If you have admitted your sin there is no longer anything you need to fear. God loves you in your brokenness, forgives you, and wants to restore fellowship with you again.

- The sacrifice acceptable to God is a broken spirit; a broken and contrite heart, O God, thou wilt not despise. Ps 51.17

We are all responsible for what kind of relationship we have with God. It isn't him that has moved away from you. Stop avoiding God and take responsibility to repair your relationship with him.

SEEDS OF HONESTY

Search your heart and expose any lies that you have been telling yourself and God. Have you been justifying your behaviour saying, "It's not so bad, there are lots of worse sins"? Have you been believing that no real harm is done if no one finds out about it? Have you been reassuring yourself that it's not really an addiction, that you could stop anytime? Have you been saying, "That's the last time, I won't do it again." Have you been putting off working on this until some point in the future? Have you been telling yourself it's not possible to change, that the urges are too strong? The first step in stopping a sin is exposing the lie that is behind it. Stop lying to yourself and instead be honest with yourself.

SEEDS OF ACCOUNTABILITY

One day each one of us will have to give account to God for the life we have lived and for how obedient we have been.
*   For we shall all stand before the judgment seat of God…each of us shall give account of himself to God. Rom 14.10 & 12

   This is not just a Bible verse. This is a promise from eternal God and it's going to happen. We will be each held personally accountable for our actions. Standing before God we will not be able to cast blame for our own moral failures. We won't be able to blame our: parents, families, teachers, churches, and even those who may have harmed us. He knows that despite even terrible trauma any life surrendered to him can be healed and made whole. Regardless of who has influenced us God still holds us accountable. No one can force us to go against God's will. Stop blaming and take responsibility for the choices you have made.

SEEDS OF OWNERSHIP

We like to tell ourselves that if only our lives had been different we wouldn't have turned out this way. Perhaps a better childhood, better health, or a better marriage would have kept us away from darkness. Is this really true? Do people with charmed lives sin less? Do people with lots of hardship sin more? The truth is that we are always responsible for our own sin and there isn't any excuse. The life you have is the one you have built. It didn't happen accidentally or outside your control. It's the result of you getting whatever you have wanted the most. All of us pursue what

47

we desire the most. Where our treasure is, there will our heart be also. We either treasure God's will, or our own selfish ends; and we end up with the inevitable result.

- What the wicked dreads will come upon him but the desire of the righteous will be fulfilled. Pr 10.24

The Bible has a very different view of sexual addiction than society's current thinking. It insists that the root of addiction is sin and not sickness. You can search the Bible from stem to stern and you will not find immoral behaviour ever referred to as a sickness. A sickness is out of our control and we do not choose it; this is why God is so compassionate with the sick. But the Bible labels sexual immorality as a sin, which means we have chosen the behaviour and are therefore held personally responsible for it. If our sin has grown into an addiction this is simply the result of our continued unrepentance. When we choose to repeatedly give in to any sin we surrender our control and suffer addiction as a consequence.

- Truly, truly, I say to you, everyone who commits sin is a slave to sin. Jn 8.34

Let's stop deluding ourselves; God has never had tolerance or compassion for unrepentant sexual sin. With God there are no excuses for sexual misconduct. In fact, if we choose to make it our practice, our very salvation is in jeopardy.

- Put to death therefore what is earthly in you: fornication, impurity, passion, evil desire and covetousness which is idolatry. On account of these the wrath of God is coming. Col 3.5
- Be sure of this, that no fornicator or impure man, or one who is covetous, (that is, an idolater) has any inheritance in the kingdom of Christ and of God. Eph 5.5
- Do you not know that the unrighteous will not inherit the kingdom of God? Do not be deceived, neither the immoral, nor idolaters, nor adulterers, nor sexual perverts. 1st Cor 6.9

It is a good thing to be frightened by the truth. Yes scripture tells you that you are in more danger than you realized, but it also tells you that you are not doomed to live a life of defeat. There is a way, but only one way to get free of sin. You can't cast it out, you

48

can't counsel it out, you can't church it out. You just have to stop making excuses and grow up. You must acknowledge that you are the one responsible for the sexual sin in your life, and you are the one responsible for putting a stop to it.

NOTES

_____

_____

_____

_____

_____

_____

_____

_____

_____

_____

_____

_____

_____

_____

_____

_____

_____

_____

_____

Step 7: Confess

Ash Pits

One of the most dangerous hazards forest fire crews face are the hidden ash pits that form whenever an intense wildfire is burning. Flames race through the tree tops and run over the ground, but they also feed on fuel under the ground. As a tree is being consumed above ground its root system also is being turned to ash. When this happens to a large tree a deep pit of ash can form. The tree itself can be gone without a trace but the ash pit remains. With all the burnt and gray debris covering the forest floor these pits are very hard to detect. It is quite possible for a crew member to stumble into a pit with ash well over his head and suffocate. The fire fighters' best defence is to work in close teams so that help is always near. Falling into sexual addiction is like falling into one of these ash pits. We fall and then find we aren't able to struggle out on our own. We are in real danger of suffocating spiritually. We feel ashamed to admit we're in trouble and are reluctant to call out for help. To get free from the pit however one has to humble themselves and ask for assistance, there is no other way. Confessing our failure and defeat to a trusted comrade is the helping hand that rescues us from the hole.

"This is a people robbed and plundered, they are all of them trapped in holes."
—Isa 42.22

Let Go of Secrecy

How many Christians remain trapped in sexual addiction because they refuse to expose their sin and ask for help?

Confession is admitting to another who we really are. It strips us of all our lies and the false persona we portray. It is incredibly humbling and our flesh hates it. For many it is the most difficult step in recovery but it is this step that seems to break the back of sexual addiction. All sin thrives in darkness and concealment; it is our shame that keeps the thing hidden. But if we are serious about taking back our life from the shadows then our sin must be exposed.

- Take no part in the unfruitful works of darkness, but instead expose them. Eph 4.11

Confessing to God alone doesn't bring our sin out into the light. God has known about it all along. We need to confess our sins not only to God, but also to a person. Confessing your sins is probably one of the hardest things you will ever do. It takes a real death to self and a decision to follow God at any cost. Being willing to swallow this bitter medicine and humble yourself shows how serious you are about defeating your own fleshy nature.

- And they were baptized by him in the river Jordan, confessing their sins. Mt 3.6

WHAT GOOD DOES CONFESSION DO?

1) CLEANSING

People who muster up the courage to confess report feelings of relief. There is a release from guilt and shame when the truth comes out. They experience mercy and a sense that God is pleased with them.

- He who conceals his transgressions will not prosper, but he who confesses and forsakes them will obtain mercy. Pr 28.13
- Lying lips are an abomination to the Lord, those who deal truthfully are his delight. Pr 12.22
- If we say we have no sin, we deceive ourselves, and the truth is not in us. If we confess our sins, He is faithful and just, and will forgive our sins and cleanse us from all unrighteousness. 1 Jn 1.9

2) HEALING

Scripture also draws clear correlations between concealed sin and poor health. It seems that carrying guilt around inside is not good for our bodies.

- When I declared not my sin my body wasted away. Ps 32.3
- There is no soundness in my flesh because of thy indignation, there is no health in my bones because of my sin. Ps 38.3
- Shun immorality. Every other sin which a man commits is outside the body; but the immoral man sins against his own body. 1st Cor 6.18

God honours honesty, and those who make the good confession will find improvements in their emotional and physical health.

- He that would love life and see good days, let him keep his tongue from evil and his lips from speaking guile. 1st Pet 3.10
- Therefore confess your sins to one another and pray for one another that you may be healed. Jam 5.16

3) FELLOWSHIP

It is a strange phenomenon, but the things we fear most about confession (rejection, humiliation, and ridicule) are the opposite of how our true brothers and sisters react. Everyone has had their own struggles with darkness and people respect the courage it takes to admit failure. True fellowship results from humbly needing one another. It's not our strengths that draw us together, but our weaknesses. Confession doesn't separate, but brings believers closer.

- If we walk in the light, as he is in the light, then we have fellowship with one another. 1st Jn 1.7

WHAT IF I'M NOT WILLING?

God wants us to confess our sins to one another for our own good. He convicts us of its necessity and provides us opportunity. It is however our choice. As always we can either choose to obey him, or choose to keep our lie hidden. What we need to realize though is that if we choose to disobey, God will not let it go. Whenever we don't listen to his instructions he always moves on to action. In order to save your spirit God will not hesitate to punish your flesh. If you tell yourself that by just keeping quiet no one will ever know, then you have forgotten who God is. God is a just God who keeps track of lies. The Bible clearly warns that if we won't expose our sin then he'll find a way to do it.

- He flatters himself in his own eyes that his iniquity cannot be found out and hated. Ps 36.2
- Though his hatred be covered with guile, his wickedness will be exposed to the assembly. Pr 26.26
- He who walks in integrity walks securely, but he who perverts his ways will be found out. Pr 10.9

God is a God of light in whom there is no darkness. Its only a matter of time before that light searches you out. You might as well get the truth out now because it's coming out sooner or later and that is a promise from God.

WHO DO I CONFESS TO?

It's important to choose wisely who you take into your confidence. Firstly make sure that it is somebody who is part of the body of Christ.

- Therefore rejecting all falsity and being done now with it, let every one express the truth with his neighbour, for we are all parts of one body and members one of another. Eph 4.25

Secondly choose someone who has reached a state of mature spirituality and isn't still living according to the flesh, or under the control of a sexual addiction.

- Brethren if any man is overtaken in any trespass, you who are spiritual should restore him in a spirit of gentleness. Gal 6.1

Thirdly choose someone who possesses humility, someone who is still aware of their own weaknesses and need for Christ.

- Bear one another's burdens and so fulfill the law of Christ. For if anyone thinks he is something, when he is nothing, he deceives himself. Gal 6. 2-3

Finally choose someone who you can count on to be confidential and never betray your trust.

- He who goes about as a talebearer reveals secrets, but he who is trustworthy in spirit keeps a thing hidden. Pr 11.13

Being a child of the light means letting go of secrecy and the false sense of security it provides. It means becoming like Jesus Christ and deciding to have nothing more to do with lies for the rest of your life.

- You are a chosen race, a royal priesthood, a holy nation, God's own people, that you may declare the wonderful deeds of him who called you out of darkness into his marvellous light. 1st Pet 2.9

NOTES

_____

_____

_____

_____

_____

_____

_____

_____

_____

_____

_____

_____

_____

_____

_____

_____

Step 8: Repent

Crown Fire

A crown fire is a very dangerous rank 5 fire which has left the ground and is raging through the forest canopy. It roars like a jet plane as flames shoot a hundred feet into the air above the trees. It creates a choking pall of black to copper coloured smoke and if a person is caught in its path it cannot be outrun. For firefighters normal ground attack strategies are ineffective because the crown fire easily leaps across hand made firebreaks. This is where the phrase "fighting fire with fire" originates. Fire crews must deliberately burn wide swaths of perfectly good forest in front of the advancing fire in what is called a controlled burn. The only way to stop a crown fire is to rob it of fuel. In a similar way Christians who want to be free of sexual addiction must take drastic steps to get control of the fire in their life. A partial repentance or half hearted commitment will only serve as a temporary blockade. To defeat sexual addiction there can no longer be any compromises with sin; an addict must renounce it completely. They must embrace a "victory at any cost" attitude, and be willing to offer their flesh as a sacrifice to be consumed by God's all consuming controlled burn.

"I appeal to you therefore brethren by the mercies of God, to present your bodies as a living sacrifice, holy and acceptable to God."

— Rom 12.1

It takes the holy fire of repentance to combat the fires of lust. We must reach a place where we will give up anything to become Christ like.

"And he who is left in Zion and remains in Jerusalem will be called holy, everyone who has been recorded for life in Jerusalem, when the Lord shall have washed away the filth of the daughters of Zion and cleansed the bloodstains of Jerusalem from its midst by a spirit of judgement and a spirit of burning." Isa 4.3-4

Let Go Of Compromise

Repentance is a word packed with negative connotations that bring up images of hell-fire evangelists trying to scare people into heaven, but what does the word actually mean? The word itself "metanoia" simply means to have a change of heart or mind. It means to be going in one direction, change your mind, and start heading in a different direction. Even God has had moments of repentance.

- When God saw what they did, how they turned from their evil way, God repented of the evil which he said he would do to them; and he did not do it. Jon 3.10

We know that repentance does not make us perfect or remove our old sinful nature. People who have had a genuine change of direction still fail and make mistakes. We are all still sinners, every one of us.

- For we all make many mistakes. Jam 3.2

So what is the difference between a sinner who has repented and one who hasn't? Think of life as a path that we are all on. In one direction the path leads toward God, in the other direction the path leads away from God. There are also side paths leading off the main one which are detours. At any given point in our life we are either walking facing toward God, walking away from him with our backs turned, or down some detour where we are partly facing him and partly turned away. There are also obstacles all along these paths regardless of what direction we are heading in. People heading away from God stumble over them, but so do people heading toward him. Repentance does not mean a life with no stumbles. A repentant heart is a heart turned toward God and seeking his will.

Our churches are full of Christians who at first zealously pursued God but have since ended up wandering down detours and have lost their thirst for him.

- But my people have forgotten me, they burn incense to false gods; they have stumbled in their ways in the ancient roads, and have gone into bypaths, and not the highway. Jer 18.13
- But I have this against you, that you have abandoned the love you had at first. Rev 2.4

These side paths are really paths of compromise. We choose them because we are in two minds about Jesus Christ. We don't want to completely turn our back on him, risk our salvation, and return to a sinner's life. But we also don't want to completely surrender our selves and live fully obedient to God. So we choose a life of compromise, a life that is half spiritual and half carnal.

- And Elijah came near to all the people, and said, "How long will you go limping with two different opinions? If the Lord is God, follow him; but if Baal then follow him. 1st Ki 18.21

This double-minded condition is the same one that Jesus addresses in the church of Laodicea in the book of Revelation.

- I know your works: you are neither cold nor hot. Would that you were either cold or hot. So, because you are lukewarm, and neither cold nor hot, I will spew you out of my mouth. Rev 3. 15-16

The word translated spew is actually the word for vomit. Suffice it to say that God finds a compromised Christian very distasteful. Jesus still loves this person, but he is not pleased with them. He counsels them to recover their zeal for him and repent from the heart.

- Those whom I love I reprove and chasten; so be zealous and repent. Rev 3.19

A friend of mine once admitted that he was a luke-warm Christian, and went on to shrug his shoulders and say that all the Christians he knew were lukewarm as well. Many are lulled into complacency because those around them aren't living obedient lives. They feel a false sense of security because it seems that luke-warmness has no real consequence. To justify their compromised state they dilute the high standards of holiness championed in scripture. They have fallen asleep spiritually. They have chosen to disregard how repugnant sin is to God.

God is a righteous judge, and a God who has indignation every day. If a man does not repent, God will whet his sword. Ps 7.11-12

There are none so blind as those who sleep. Is this you? Shake yourself from this drowsiness. Remember that God calls us to purity and holiness. God's word clearly states what he expects of us morally.

GOD'S STANDARD OF HOLINESS — EYE SALVE FOR THE SLEEPING

- As obedient children do not be conformed to the passions of your former ignorance, but as he who called you is holy, be holy yourselves in all your conduct; since it is written, "You shall be holy, for I am holy." 1st Pet 1. 14-16
- But I say walk by the Spirit and do not gratify the desires of the flesh. Gal 5.16
- Everyone who looks at a woman lustfully has already committed adultery with her in his heart. Mt 5.28
- But rather I wrote to you not to associate with anyone who bears the name of brother if he is guilty of immorality, not even to eat with such a one. 1st Cor 5.11
- Let marriage, be held in honour among all, and let the marriage bed be undefiled; for God will judge the immoral and adulterous. Heb 13.4
- Can one walk upon hot coals and his feet not be scorched? So is he who goes into his neighbour's wife; none who touches her will go unpunished. Pr 6.28
- For I tell you that unless your righteousness exceeds that of the scribes and Pharisees, you will never enter the kingdom of heaven. Mt 5.20
- Little children let no one deceive you. He who does right is righteous as he is righteous. He who commits sin {continues to make

58

sin his practice} is of the devil; for the devil has sinned from the beginning. The reason the Son of God appeared was to destroy the works of the devil. 1st Jn 3. 7-8

If we are fully turned toward God in our hearts, sin will not be our habit. We will still struggle with sin, but we will be repentant sinners. When we do stumble on occasion, there will be grace and not judgment.

- As far as the east is from the west, so far does he remove our transgressions from us. As a father pities his children, so the Lord pities those who fear him. Ps 103.12-13
- I will remember their sins and their misdeeds no more. Heb 10.17

If however we are unrepentant sinners, God treats our sin differently. If we are deliberately turning our back on God, or if we are killing time down the detour of luke-warm Christianity, we won't escape God's discipline. He will not be so unjust as to treat us the same way as the ones who have had the courage to repent. There is every reason for us to fear God; Christians are not immune to God's judgment. Just because we are saved does not mean we get away with deliberate and persistent sin.

- For if we sin deliberately after receiving the knowledge of the truth, there no longer is a sacrifice for sins, but a fearful prospect of judgment. Heb 10.26-27
- And all the churches shall know that I am he who searches mind and heart, and I will give to each of you as your works deserve. Rev 2.23
- For the wrongdoer will be paid back for the wrong he has done, and there is no partiality. Col 3.25

Don't be lulled into thinking that God's judgment is far off, something in the distant future at judgment day that you don't have to worry about now. God's discipline is also carried out today.

- For the time has come for judgment to begin with the household of God; 1st Pet 4.17
- But they will give account to him who is ready to judge the living and the dead. 1st Pet 4.5

- I will chasten you in just measure, and I will by no means leave you unpunished. Jer 30.11

Don't believe the widespread lie that salvation excuses us from holiness. The gospel has always been a call to personal change. Salvation is not at all unconditional; it has always comes with a requirement. Without repentance there is no forgiveness for sins.

- Do you presume upon the riches of his kindness and forbearance, and patience? Do you not know that God's kindness is meant to lead you to repentance? Rom 2.4
- For I did not come to call the righteous, but sinners to repentance. Mt 9.13
- I tell you, No; unless you repent you will all likewise perish. Lk 13.5
- Repent therefore and be converted that your sins may be blotted out, so that times of refreshing may come from the presence of the Lord. Acts 3.19

If you are an unrepentant Christian you are already under some form of God's discipline. If you are honest with yourself you will see that your life has plenty of indications of being unblessed.

- Now therefore thus says the Lord of hosts: consider how you have fared: you have sown much, and harvested little; you eat, but you never have enough; you drink, but you never have your fill; you clothe yourselves but no one is warm; he who earns wages, earns wages to put them into a bag with holes …You have looked for much, and lo, it came to little, and when you brought it home, I blew it away. Hag 1. 5-6 & 9

In this state you cannot expect deliverance from bondage. In fact you cannot expect improvement in any area of your life. And it doesn't matter how crowded it is down that detour path of compromise. The fact that you are surrounded by so many luke-warm Christians does not make you less accountable to God. To God repentance is not negotiable. God does not expect perfection, but he does expect genuine repentance. In order to receive the power to change your life you must first change your mind. He is full of mercy and is so willing to help, but you must do your part. Repentance has always been the remedy for sin. Change your direction and he will work with you to change your life.

- "Therefore I will judge you O house of Israel, everyone according to his ways," says the Lord God. Repent and turn away from all your transgressions so that iniquity will not be your ruin. Ezek 18.30
- Work out your own salvation with fear and trembling, for God is at work in you. Phil 2.12

Meditation verses:

Mt 4.17, 1st Thess 4.3-8, 2nd Cor 7.1, Heb 12.28-29, Heb 12.11-14, 1st Pet 1.14-16, Col 3. 5-6, Heb 13.4, Eph 5. 5-6, Eph 4. 22-24

NOTES

Step 9: Give

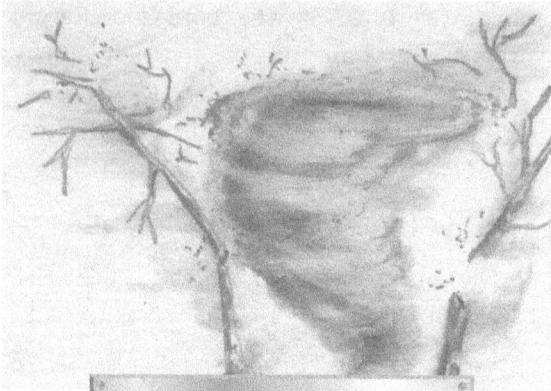

Firestorm

When conditions are right for a wildfire to grow out of control a fire storm may develop. A fire storm is a feature of a rank 6 fire and is considered too dangerous to fight. It occurs when a forest fire is so intense that it makes it's own wind. Any fire requires air because fire burns oxygen. A large wildfire requires a great deal of air and it sucks this air towards itself from the surrounding countryside. This creates strong surface inflow winds of up to 160 km/hr, strong enough to knock over trees. These rushing winds roar toward the center of the fire from all points of the compass, feeding the fire with loose oxygen. At the core of the conflagration temperatures can reach 2000 degrees, hot enough to melt metal. The superheated air at the center roars upwards in powerful updrafts, so strong that they begin to rotate and form fire whirls. (also called fire devils) These are whirling vortexes of fire too powerful to be extinguished; these are fire storms.

"Three things are never satisfied; four which never say, "Enough.": Sheol, the barren womb, the earth ever thirsty for water, and the fire which never says, "Enough."

— Pr 30.16

Like a fire storm, a sexual addict tends to draw everything in his life towards himself. He is never satisfied and is self-indulgent at the core, everything revolves around him and his needs. His lust is a kind of greed, and he is indifferent to the needs of those around him. When he is feeding his addiction those who happen to be in his vicinity are in danger. The more advanced his addiction the more harm he will inflict. To be free of addiction we must become free of our vortex of greed! We must renounce being the center of our world, and practice how to put others needs ahead of our own. In the end, it is love that robs lust of its power.

Let Go of Selfishness

The root of sexual sin is greed, or what the bible terms coveting. This is simply the desire for something that does not belong to you.

- You shall not covet your neighbour's house; you shall not covet your neighbour's wife, or his manservant, or his maidservant, or his ox, or his ass, or anything that is your neighbour's. Ex 20.17
- But fornication and all impurity or covetousness must not even be named among you as is fitting among saints. Eph 5.3

Whether it is sinning with your eyes, thoughts, or behaviour, all sexual sin is about taking and not about giving. If you look at a woman lustfully you are thinking about yourself and what you want from her. You are not thinking about her as a person at all. Lust is the opposite of love. Sex addicts are very self absorbed and become so focused on their own need that they become blind to how disrespectfully they are treating others. They can do real harm to others' lives in what can become a reckless pursuit of their own gratification.

- They have eyes full of adultery, insatiable for sin. They entice unsteady souls. They have hearts trained in greed. Accursed children! Forsaking the right way they have gone astray; 2nd Pet 2.14-15

Just as the roots of a plant provide it with nutrition and support it is the root of sexual addiction that keeps it fed. When we begin to understand that underneath every sexual addiction is a deep root of greed, we are getting close to exposing the truth about immorality. Our covetousness is actually a form of idolatry.

- Be sure of this, that no fornicator or impure man, or one who is covetous (that is, an idolater), has any inheritance in the kingdom of Christ and of God. Eph 5.5

When I choose sexual addiction, I put myself up on a throne above others and above God. I create an idol out of myself and put the dictates and demands of self above all. Within every sex addict is an overindulged and demanding flesh used to getting what it wants. Without confronting and overthrowing this idol of self, you will remain ever enslaved to it. You must expose your greed for what it really is, a god in place of God, and a terrible enemy to your recovery. This idol is something that God would love you to hate, but idols are typically very well cared for. The list below describes the typical ways we indulge our idols.

PROPER IDOL CARE & MAINTENANCE

1) Set up - Son of man, these men have set up their idols in their hearts, and put before them that which causes them to stumble into iniquity. Ezek 14.3

2) Conceal - Then he said to me, Son of man, have you seen what the elders of the house of Israel do in the dark, every man in his secret chamber of idols? Ezek 8.12

3) Attach Yourself - Ephraim is joined fast to idols, so let him alone to take the consequences. Hos 4.17

4) Bow Down to - And they followed other gods from the people who were all around them, and they bowed down to them; and they provoked the Lord to anger. Judg 2.12

5) Depend on - And the rest of it he makes into a god, his carved image. He falls down before it and worships it, prays to it and says, " Deliver me, for you are my god!" Isa 44.17

6) Sacrifice for - The more I called them, the more they went from me; they kept sacrificing to the Baals, and burning incense to idols. Hos 11.2

7) Adore - Those who lavish gold from the purse and weigh out silver in the scales, hire a goldsmith, and he makes it into a god; then they fall down and worship. Isa 46.6

To free yourself from sexual addiction you will have to destroy the idol of greed, but be prepared for opposition from your flesh. It will not give up the selfish life without a fight. To choose to live unselfishly is to stop catering to self. It means making the self uncomfortable and denying it control. It means reversing the process of nourishing and supporting greed, and taking the steps necessary to weaken and destroy it. These steps are listed below.

- Put to death therefore what is earthly in you: fornication, impurity, passion, evil desire, and covetousness which is idolatry. Col 3.5

IDOL REMOVAL
1) Call For A Doctor

When we love and obey something more than God, (even if that something is ourselves) then we have set up an idol in our hearts. We've placed it in an exalted position; we've set it up on a high place within us.

- For they also built for themselves high places, sacred pillars, and wooden images on every high hill and under every green tree. 1 Ki 14.23

Once installed, idols demand complete submission! They immediately set about erasing God's commands he has written on our hearts, starting with the first.

- You shall have no other god's before me. Ex 20.3

They then write their own replacement set of commandments on our hearts.

- The sin of Judah is written with a pen of iron; with a point of diamond it is engraved on the tablet of their heart. Jer 17.1

To remove an idol that has gained control you are going to need God's help. Trying to do it by yourself would be like trying to remove your own malignant tumour. You're going to need a skilled surgeon to complete this operation successfully.

- I will sprinkle clean water upon you, and you shall be clean from all your uncleannesses, and from all your idols I will cleanse you. A new heart I will give you and a new spirit I will put within you; and I will take out of your flesh your heart of stone; Ezek 36.25-26

Turn to the great physician.

2) *Expose*

Idols thrive in the dark. It was not enough that the house of Israel hid their idolatry behind closed doors. Their idols were doubly concealed, for even the door to their secret chamber was plastered over.

- And he brought me to the door of the court; and when I looked, behold, there was a hole in the wall. Then he said to me, son of man, dig now in the wall. And when I had dug in the wall, behold, there was a door. And he said to me, go in and see the wicked abominations that they do here. Ezek 8. 7-9

Remember that hidden behind sexual addiction is greed. Lust cannot thrive without coveting and selfishness. This is the real idol in your life that must be exposed and brought out into the light. Ask the Holy Spirit to bring to your attention any time you are being selfish. Deliberately focus your attention on catching yourself having a "me first" attitude. Examine how you are with money, chores, relationships, and all your various activities. You will see that your sexual greed is only the tip of the iceberg. It is through being willing to open your eyes that God's light will enter you. Like pulling back the curtains, opening your eyes to the truth allows light to permeate your own secret chamber. Your idol will soon start to feel quite uncomfortable.

- The eye is the light {transparent window} of the body. So, if your eye is single {clear} your whole body will be full of light. Mt 6.22

Ruthlessly search your life for selfishness.

3) *Detach*

We are very attached to our idols, especially if our idol is our own self. It feels natural to weigh everything we do in terms of how it will benefit us.

- These are blemishes on your love feasts, as they boldly carouse together, looking after themselves; Jude 12

Putting yourself first may be natural, but it is not spiritual. The

Holy Spirit wants to free us form all forms of greed.

- They have become callous and given themselves up to licentiousness, greedy to practice every kind of uncleanness. You did not so learn Christ! Eph 4.19-20

Sometimes we forget the Holy Spirit's intention is to make us like Jesus Christ.

- Now the Lord is the Spirit and where the Spirit of the lord is, there is freedom. And we all, with unveiled face, beholding the glory of the Lord, are being changed into his likeness from one degree of glory to another; 2nd Cor 3.17-18

Jesus Christ did not put himself and his needs first. If we are becoming Christ-like we must relinquish selfishness and become willing to live a different way.

- Let each of us please his neighbour for his good, to edify him. For Christ did not please himself. Rom 15.2-3
- Have this mind amongst yourselves which is yours in Christ Jesus, who, though he was in the form of God did not count equality with God a thing to be grasped, but emptied himself, taking the form of a servant. Phil 2.5-7

Jesus did not count equality with God a thing to be grasped. Unlike billions of us grasping and getting every day, Jesus didn't grasp for anything. He did not put his will on par with God's; he did not set his self up as an idol. He emptied himself of his self, and made it his goal in life to enrich others' lives. He put others' fulfillment ahead of his own. Jesus Christ was content to be a servant. We have the choice to do the same. We can relinquish a self-serving and self-absorbed life and choose to adopt his life style. We detach from selfishness by becoming attached to service.

- Do nothing from selfishness or conceit, but in humility count others better than yourselves. Let each of you look not only to his own interests but also to the interests of others. Phil 2.3-4

We can choose to use the talents God has given us for the benefit of others.

- As each has received a gift, employ it for one another, as good stewards of God's varied grace. 1st Pet 4.10

If we make this decision, to renounce the kingdom of self, we will discover a whole new freedom and power over sin. A giving person makes for a reluctant sinner and a terrible sex addict.

Detach from the rule of self by embracing the service of others.

4) *Choose Faith*

Confronting an idol takes courage. They are powerful and don't like being challenged. Sometimes it seems easier to not disturb them, even if it means a life of continued slavery. In Moses' time the children of Israel were under bondage to taskmasters, and then God promised them a new land; a land of peace and rest and freedom from slavery.

- I have seen the affliction of my people who are in Egypt, and have heard their cry because of their taskmasters; I know their sufferings, and have come down to deliver them out of the hand of the Egyptians, and to bring them up out of that land to a good and broad land, a land flowing with milk and honey. Ex 3.7-8

Even though God promised this land to them, the people discovered that he wasn't going to hand it to them on a silver platter. They were going to have to fight for it. After their long march from Egypt, at the border of Canaan, they sent spies to check out the land; the spies however reported a minor obstacle - giants!

- The land, through which we have gone, to spy it out, is a land that devours its inhabitants; and all the people that we saw in it are men of great stature. And there we saw the Nephilim; and we seemed to ourselves like grasshoppers, and so we seemed to them. Num 13.32-33

The prospect of having to fight against giants drew two distinct responses from the children of Israel; on the one hand cowardice, and on the other courage.

1) Then the men who had gone up with him said, " We are not able to go up against the people; for they are stronger than we." Num 13.31

2) But Caleb quieted the people before Moses, and said, "Let us

go up at once, and occupy it, for we are well able to overcome it." Num 13.30

Feeling fear is not a sin. Both timid and brave people feel fear, but they differ in their response to it. Why did the majority of the people collapse in fear? What allowed Joshua and Caleb to stand up to it? Joshua reveals, in his argument for invasion, what his courage was based on.

- "If the Lord delights in us, he will bring us into this land and give it to us, a land which flows with milk and honey. Only, do not rebel against the Lord; and do not fear the people of the land, for they are bread for us; their protection is removed from them, and the Lord is with us; do not fear them. Num 14.8-9

If we feel we are faced with fighting giants on our own, it's no wonder we retreat. In our mind we know we can't win. Joshua believed that God was with him and would fight for him. The secret to Joshua and Caleb's courage was their faith.

Courage is not an emotion. Courage is a choice to put trust in God. Cowardice is also not an emotion but a choice; a choice to not put trust in God.

- How long will this people despise me? And how long will they not believe in me, in spite of all the things which I have wrought amongst them? Num 14.11
- And to whom did he swear that they should never enter his rest, but to those who were disobedient? So we see that they were unable to enter because of unbelief. Heb 3. 18-19

Joshua and Caleb believed not only that God was with them, but that he was with them as a dread warrior. They believed that God would empower them and weaken their enemies.

- Know therefore this day that he who goes over before you as a devouring fire is the Lord your God; he will destroy them and subdue them before you; so you shall drive them out and make them perish quickly, as the Lord has promised you. Deut 9.3

For those trying to find the courage to take on the inner giant of selfishness and sexual greed, do they have such a promise? Can they put their faith in a God who will fight for them?

- What then shall we say to this? If God is for us, who is against us? He who did not spare his own Son, but gave him up for us all, will he not also give us all things with him? Rom 8.31
- I will not leave you desolate; I will come to you. Jn 14.18

Do we think that the same person who gave up his life for us would abandon us in our battle with the flesh? Jesus will fight for your freedom; he died for it. His whole reason for coming was to free you from bondage and see you into your own promised land.

- The reason the Son of God appeared was to destroy the works of the devil. 1st Jn 3.8
- I came that they may have life and have it abundantly. Jn 10.10

Your job is to believe, and then you too can stand up to giants and inherit what is rightfully yours.

- For whatever is born of God overcomes the world; and this is the victory that overcomes the world, our faith. 1st Jn 5.4
- For thou didst gird me with strength for the battle; thou didst make my assailants sink under me. Ps 18.39

Choose faith, and you'll find courage.

5) Stop Depending on It

Keeping an idol has secondary benefits. Let's face it, if it wasn't meeting some need we wouldn't maintain it. Life is full of struggle, disappointment, and difficulty, and this affects us emotionally. We all experience feelings of discouragement, anxiety, loneliness, and sadness. God wants us to come close to him at these times because he is drawn to us when we are hurting.

- The Lord is near to the broken-hearted and saves the crushed in spirit. Ps 34.18

The Holy Spirit is our comforter. He knows us intimately, and is well equipped to both console and counsel.

- I will pray the Father, and he will give you another comforter to be with you forever, even the Spirit of truth. Jn 14.16

But when we are hurting we find it difficult to turn only to the

Spirit for help. It is when we are weak that we are most tempted to take things into our own hands to try to find some relief but God wants to be the one to quench our thirst.

- For my people have committed two evils; they have forsaken me, the fountain of living waters, and hewed out cisterns for themselves, broken cisterns, that can hold no water. Jer 2.13

It saddens God when we won't rely on him in our need. Scripture says he loves us like a husband. He is trustworthy if we would just trust him, but we keep looking to our own flesh for deliverance. He regards this as a kind of adultery.

- Go again, love a woman who is loved by a lover and is committing adultery, just like the love of the Lord for the children of Israel, who look to other gods. Hos 3.1

God has promised countless times in scripture that we can rely on him and yet we are so reluctant to take this risk. This has an effect on God.

- What shall I do with you, O Ephraim? What shall I do with you, O Judah? Your love is like a morning cloud, like the dew that goes early away. Hos 6.4

David understood that when we cave into the flesh to satisfy our need we are really declaring that God is not worthy of our trust.

- Against thee, thee only, have I sinned, and done that which is evil in thy sight. Ps 51.4

Our discomfort is really an opportunity for us to demonstrate our trust in him. Our need is really a chance to bless him. How gladdening it would be to God if we refused the "quick fix" solutions of the flesh, and turned to him in our need. This does mean however that we may have to wait a while in discomfort. Sometimes God does deliver us from trouble, but more often he delivers us through it.

- Your adversary the devil prowls around like a roaring lion, seeking someone to devour. Resist him, firm in your faith, knowing that the same experience of suffering is required of your brotherhood throughout the world. And after you have suffered a little while, the God of grace, who has called you to his eternal glory in Christ, will himself, restore, establish, and strengthen you. 1st Pet 5.6-10

In our affluent society we have a low tolerance for pain and difficulty. We seem to lack resilience and are easily overwhelmed. Our pleasure-based culture promises us quick fixes for any problem we might have. This is not how the kingdom of God works. God does not view our suffering as an inconvenience to be quickly removed. To him pain is a teacher with many valuable lessons to impart. He knows that if we live risk-free and pain-free lives our character will never develop.

- More than that, we rejoice in our suffering, knowing that suffering produces endurance, and endurance produces character, and character produces hope. Rom 5.3-4

We are faced with an important choice between self or God as our rescuer. If we look to our idol of self to deliver us we can receive quick relief, but it is only a temporary solution. We may feel better but we aren't getting any better. The problem has not gone away, the unpleasant feelings will soon return. If we look to God as our deliverer we won't find immediate relief. We will have to bear with discomfort while we wait for him, but he will gradually teach us the way out and his solution will be permanent.

- Many are the afflictions of the righteous; but the Lord delivers him out of them all. Ps 34.19

Stop looking for the quick fix and tolerate a little discomfort.

6) Stop Sacrificing Your Life for it

In the ancient world people made idols to represent whatever god they worshiped. In most cultures it was common to make sacrifices to these idols. A sacrifice was simply a gift offered to a deity and these gifts were offered upon raised platforms called altars. The idea of the sacrifice was that you offered something valuable, something that came at a personal cost to you. The reason for a sacrifice was typically to appease a god. If people felt that their god was upset with them they would give him something to calm him down and avoid his ire. Although no longer carved from stone, idols and their altars are still with us. Now they reside inside our hearts and minds. And we still make sacrifices to them. We lay upon altars things of great value to us in order to keep our idols happy. Consider the idol of sexual addiction. We serve it, bow down to it, obey it, and even give it our adoration, but what does it cost us? What parts of our lives have we offered up and laid upon it's altar?

COSTS OF SEXUAL ADDICTION

1) Close relationship with God
2) Honest relationship with wife or fiancé
3) A clear conscience
4) Personal integrity (because of the necessity of secrets)
5) Your life's mission and calling from God
6) Risk of exposure and loss of reputation
7) Risk of consequences at work
8) Risk of reprisal from angry people
9) Risk of legal repercussions
10) Risk of falling under God's judgment

Exploring just one of the above sacrifices can illustrate just how much we seem to be willing to lay on this altar. Cost number 5 states that maintaining a sexual addiction robs you of being used by God. How do we know this?

• Be sure of this, that no fornicator, or impure man, or one who is covetous (that is, an idolater) has any inheritance in the kingdom of Christ and of God. Let no one deceive you with empty words, for it is because of these things that the wrath of God comes upon the sons of disobedience. Eph 5.5-6

God is choosy about who he sends to do his work. Such a person must re-present Christ in love and also in purity.

• If anyone purifies himself from what is ignoble, then he will be a vessel for noble use, consecrated and useful to the master of the house, ready for any good work. 2nd Tim 2.21

Don't be taken in by any watered-down Christianity which

tells you that holiness is no longer required. Read your Bible and you will see that God still expects holiness.

- For they disciplined us for a short time at their pleasure, but he disciplines us for our good, that we may share his holiness. Heb 12.10
- Strive for peace with all men, and for the holiness without which no one will see the Lord. Heb 12.14

The Holy Spirit does not engage the flesh to accomplish his work. If we live according to the dictates of the flesh we can't be responsive to the leading of the Spirit. To be used by the Spirit we must walk in the Spirit; to walk in the Spirit we must be holy and obedient.

- The unspiritual man does not receive the things of the Spirit of God, for they are a folly to him, and he is not able to understand them for they are spiritually discerned. 1st Cor 2.14
- So shun youthful passions and aim at righteousness, faith, love, and peace, along with those who call upon the Lord from a pure heart. 2nd Tim 2.22

Whatever form of sexual addiction you are struggling with don't fool yourself; there are serious spiritual costs to you. Your idol will always demand far more from you than it will ever give you The longer you have served it, the more of your spiritual life you have sacrificed to it. Many miss God's purpose and calling for their life because of service to such an idol. The question is, is it worth it?

- He who finds his {lower} life will lose it {the higher life}, and he who loses his {lower} life for my sake will find it {the higher life}. Mt 10.39

Assess what sin is costing you.

7) Hate It

Fleshy idols are just like parasites, they suck the life out of our spirits. It is easy to understand why God hates them.

- You shall burn the carved images of their gods with fire; you shall not covet the silver or gold that is on them, nor take it for yourselves, lest you be snared by it; for it is an abomination to the Lord your God. Deut 7.25

To eliminate an idol from your life you need to come to hate it like God does. When we hate, we experience three stages of emotion. Firstly we experience a strong unpleasant feeling of DISLIKE. Next we want to put as much DISTANCE as we can between ourselves and what we hate. Thirdly we feel we want to do DAMAGE to what we hate. (These three are a perfect antonym to love. When we love someone we have pleasant feelings towards them, want to be near them, and want to benefit them somehow.) When the children of Israel invaded the land of the Canaanites, God commanded them to hate the idols they found there.

DISLIKE
- Nor shall you bring an abomination into your house, lest you be doomed to destruction like it. You shall utterly detest and utterly abhor it, for it is an accursed thing. Deut 7.26

DISTANCE
- And when the Lord your God delivers them over to you, you shall conquer them and utterly destroy them. You shall make no covenant with them or show mercy to them. Deut 7.2

DAMAGE
- But thus shall you deal with them: you shall break down their altars, and dash in pieces their pillars, and hew down their Asherim, and burn their graven images with fire. Deut 7.5

Unfortunately the people of God did not heed his instructions. They permitted a diminished practice of idolatry to exist at the periphery of their society.

- But the Canaanites persisted in dwelling in that land. When Israel grew strong they put the Canaanites to forced labour, but did not utterly drive them out. Judg 1.27-28
- And you shall make no covenants with the inhabitants of this land; you shall break down their alters. But you have not obeyed my command. What is this that you have done? Judg 2.2

God's people disobeyed his command of annihilation. They

chose the path of compromise and tolerated practices that they knew were an abomination to God. They began to become friendly with the Canaanites, even intermarrying with them. Over time God's people were drawn astray and ensnared by idolatry.

- So now I say, I will not drive them out before you; but they shall become adversaries to you, and their gods shall be a snare to you. Judg 2.3

The experience of the children of Israel is a sad allegory of what is happening to so many Christians today. Our society is awash with greed and sexual immorality. These are the gods of today. Do we hate these and want nothing to do with them, or do we tolerate them and form attachments with them?

- For whatever was written in former days was written for our instruction, that by steadfastness and the encouragement of the scripture we might have hope. Rom 15.4

If we make compromises with our idols, they will ensnare us just as they did to the children of Israel. When dealing with idols you have to be ruthless. If we permit one to occupy even a small corner of our life, we leave open the back door for sin. Many who do get free from sexual addiction fall back into it because they wouldn't commit to the sin's complete eradication. If you allow your flesh any opportunity, it will always renew its attempts to destroy your spiritual progress.

- But put on the Lord Jesus Christ, and make no provision for the flesh, to gratify its desires. Rom 13.14

Claiming your own spiritual promised land is about destroying the idols in your life. It is about mercilessly conquering anything that puts itself before God. It is about exposing the enemy within and hating it for what it has stolen from you.

- The Lord loves those who hate evil. Ps 97.10

Show no mercy to sin.

NOTES

Step 10: Make Amends

Firebrands

Large rank 5 or 6 wildfires are explosive and hurl burning debris into the air. Some of these are burning branches, thus the name "firebrand." Due to the thermal winds generated at the centre of the fire these burning missiles soar hundreds of feet into the air and are thrown out in front of the advancing fire. Where ever they land they start up new fires which in turn race back toward the main fire drawn by strong inflow winds. Being caught between such encroaching fires is a particularly deadly place for fire crews. Another dangerous projectile associated with extreme fires is the fireball. Round, basketball sized, gaseous balls of fire are launched hundreds of feet outwards from the fire center. Where they land they explode and create blazing rings of fire on the ground which also serve to ignite new fires. When someone is in the grip of an out of control sexual addiction they too send out firebrands.

"When fire breaks out and catches in thorns so that the stacked grain, or the standing grain, or the field is consumed, he that kindled the fire shall make full restitution."

Ex 22.6

Whether an addict is aware of it or not, his problem is also a problem for those in his vicinity. There are many direct and indirect ways that one person's addiction harms others; some of these are plain, some are less obvious. A recovering addict needs to face the harm that his addiction has caused and ask who has been damaged by being in the proximity of their volatile problem? Part of recovery is attempting to set right the wrong that has been done.

Let Go of Egoism

Like other addictions, sexual addiction produces victims. A recovering person needs to ask themselves if their problem has harmed anyone. This is especially challenging for people with sexual addictions because they tend to be especially focused on themselves and their own needs. They practice a form of "egoism," which is the regarding of one's own welfare as supreme. Addicts become quite skilled in justifying and excusing their behaviour to their pre-eminent self. They tell lies to themselves that permit them to continue the behaviour that they are addicted to.

-It's just pornography, I'm not exploiting anyone

-As long as she doesn't find out, there's no harm done

-It's okay to look, as long as I don't touch

-The feelings are too strong, I can't help myself

-She came on to me

-I'm only human

-I'm a Christian, God won't judge me for this

-I can handle it, it won't go any further

-This will never come out into the open

Wherever there is persistent and knowing sin, there is always a lie close at hand. This practice of lying to self becomes habitual and has a hardening effect upon our minds. We eventually become resistant to truth and don't want to hear it.

• For this people's heart has grown dull, and their ears are heavy of hearing, and their eyes they have closed. Acts 28.27

It is this lying that hardens our hearts to the impact our addiction has on those around us. The last thing a committed addict wants to think about is the effect their behaviour has had on others. Someone committing adultery doesn't consider the impact this could have on the other person's spouse or children. A person staring lustfully at a stranger doesn't think about how uncomfortable they may be making that person feel. In order to overcome sexual addiction we must reverse this habit of inconsideration. We must let go of our egoism and deliberately learn to empathize with others. We have to stop lying to ourselves, and face the truth about how we harm others in order to indulge our own sexual appetites. For many this can provide a strong motivation for change.

This recovery step is called, "making amends" and is about doing what you can to repair any injury you've caused. There are five stages to making proper amends.

1. BE HONEST WITH YOURSELF

Generally sexual addictions fall into three levels of harm beginning with level 1 behaviours and most often progressing over time. People in an addict's life fall into greater and greater risk of harm as his addiction progresses.

Level 1 - pornography, lasciviousness, compulsive masturbation etc. These behaviours are seen as victimless, but hidden forms of victimization and exploitation are often present.

Level 2 - promiscuity, adultery, child pornography, prostitution, exhibitionism, voyeurism, etc. There are always victims associated with these behaviours.

Level 3 - rape, abuse, child molestation, incest etc. These behaviours inflict serious and lasting harm to others.

Besides the direct victims of sexual addicts there are also a pool of people who are indirectly harmed. Like a stone tossed into a pond the ripple effect of sex addiction radiates out beyond the victim to include other people in their life.

Victim — Victim's Family — Victim's Friends — Community

Paul described this process when he confronted incest occurring in the Corinthian church. One person's sexual addiction always has some kind of ripple effect and is capable of causing widespread harm.

- Your boasting is not good. Do you not know that a little leaven leavens the whole lump? 1st Cor 5.6

Make an honest appraisal of your own behaviour. What level is your addiction, and what is its ripple effect? Don't make the mistake of thinking that a level 1 addiction causes no harm. What effect does compulsive masturbation and lewd fantasies have on a marriage? What effect does an unhappy marriage have on children? What effect do lusting eyes have on women and their sense of dignity? What impact do Christian men looking at pornography have on the exploitation of teenage girls? What effect does Christian men watching pornographic videos have on Jesus, when the women in these videos are the very ones he is trying to rescue from histories of abuse?

2. FEEL REMORSE

If you are honest with yourself about the effect your addiction has had on others, you will feel remorse. This is a step in the right direction. This is conviction of sin, or as Paul called it, "godly grief." Not all guilt is bad; remorse is a good guilt that can help lead to change.

- As it is I rejoice, not because you were grieved, but because you were grieved into repenting; for you felt a godly grief, so that you suffered no loss through us. For godly grief produces a repentance that leads to salvation and brings no regret, but worldly grief produces death. 2 Cor 7.9

We are supposed to feel godly grief when we have done wrong. When we see that we have harmed others this guilt serves to correct our behaviour. It causes us to feel sorry for what we've done. The ability to feel remorseful is a reliable indication of a person's readiness to change. The inability to feel sorry is an indication that one is still thinking of themselves and has not yet empathized with the victim.

- Were they ashamed when they committed abomination? No, they were not at all ashamed; they did not know how to blush. Jer 6.15

We are not referring here to self-accusation and self-loathing which only serve to further discourage a person struggling with addiction. The difference between godly grief and negative self-accusation is sometimes hard to discern. Both are based upon unflattering truths about our failings, both are painful, yet one is good for us and one is destructive. How do we tell them apart? It all depends on recognizing the voice of the one who is speaking. Criticism can come from four possible sources.

A) Self-Criticism
-Our own flesh being hard on us through self talk
- And he (Elijah) asked that he might die, saying, "It is enough now, O Lord, take away my life; for I am no better than my fathers." 1st Ki 19.4

B) Satan's Criticism
-Demonic barbs aimed at us to discourage us
- Take the shield of faith with which you can quench all the flaming darts of the evil one. Eph 6.16

C) People's Criticism
-Other people's hurtful comments
- There is one whose rash words are like sword thrusts. Pr 12.18

D) God's Criticism
-Spoken out of love and for our own good
- I know O Lord that thy judgments are right, and that in faithfulness (loyalty) thou hast hurt me. Ps 119.75

If you want to know if it is God's voice speaking ask if there is love in the voice. When the Spirit of God convicts us the truth is wrapped in love. The Holy Spirit is patient, gentle, peaceful, and full of love and concern for you. When he speaks the truth he is thinking of your good.
- And the word of God became flesh and dwelt amongst us, full of grace and truth. Jn 1.14

When our own fleshy nature browbeats us, when satan accuses us, when fleshy people criticise us, there is truth in what they say, but no love. They do not speak to benefit us. This kind of criticism produces what Paul calls, "worldly grief." It causes discouragement and heaviness, and leads to spiritual decay rather than improvement. When God speaks to us, (sometimes through godly people) it leads to repentance and to spiritual rejuvenation. We can sense the love behind the discipline. It causes us to feel sorry, not just sorrow. Genuine remorse that comes from hearing God is a powerful force in helping us change.

3. ADMIT

When you have been honest with yourself, and have arrived at remorse, it is time to face the music. Make a list of the people you have harmed and be prepared to make amends. This will be difficult for you to do but you are now no longer thinking only about yourself. You are now thinking about what you can do for others. First, however, consider what you can not do.

A) You can't undo what you've done. - The tragic reality is that though you wish you could, you cannot erase the consequences your actions have had on others.

B) You can't make someone forgive you. - You must not insist on anyone's forgiveness. To forgive or not forgive is each individual's decision, and is between them and God. You may ask for forgiveness, but do not beg. Begging is a form of applying pressure, and is about your need again and not your victim's pain.

C) You can't expect reconciliation. - If you have had a relationship with the one you have harmed you might have to accept that the relationship may be over. This is also outside your control and is up to the other party to decide.

Now let's talk about what you *can* do. There are things that victims do need to hear, that can do them some good and help them recover from their injury. This will be humbling for you, but healing for them.

A) Admit what you've done. - Be honest and describe all that you've done that was wrong. Don't hold any secrets back, tell the whole truth.

B) Take responsibility - Acknowledge that you are accountable for what you did; that you chose to do things that harmed others. Do not make a single excuse. Do not attempt to make your victim understand why you did what you did.

4. APOLOGIZE

An apology is not about you. It should not include references to how bad you feel. It is simply saying that you understand the damage you have done to people's lives, and that you are genuinely sorry for it.

A) Empathize - Demonstrate that you grasp the hurt your actions have caused. List how your behaviour has negatively impacted the victim's life. Also include the ripple effect your actions have had upon other's lives.

B) Express remorse - For a victim, the words, "I am sorry" can be very freeing if they are said with sincerity.

On a practical note, you will have to prayerfully consider what is the best way to go about this. Should you make the rounds and meet people one on one? Should you gather people and speak to them in a group? Would this be better done in person or by letter? What if someone doesn't want to hear from you? Then there is the question; "What if my admission will hurt the person?" For example, the husband who has cheated on his wife. Some men tell themselves that the kinder thing to do is to keep it all a secret. For Christians, there is no scriptural basis for not confessing our sins. The Bible clearly teaches us not to have secrets. This includes telling the truth even when it is very painful to hear. Satan is the lover of lies and secrets. God is a lover of truth and light; in him is no darkness.

- Therefore, putting away falsehood, let everyone speak the truth with his neighbour, for we are members of one another. Eph 4.25

- If you are offering your gift at the altar and there remember your brother has something against you, leave your gift there before the alter and go; first be reconciled to your brother and then come and offer your gift. Mt 5.23-24

If we are not willing to admit our sin, the Bible promises that God will bring it out into the open anyway. Our secret is going to come out sooner or later and the sooner we confess it the better. This is because the longer we keep it hidden, the more traumatic and life-altering it will be for others when it's exposed. If you've reached the point where you are willing to put others' needs ahead of your own, you'll know what to do.

- Nothing is covered up that will not be revealed, or hidden that will not be known. Lk 12.2
- Your sin will find you out. Num 32.23

Seek counsel and support from a spiritually mature person before embarking on truth telling. You want to go about this wisely, in a way that will do the greatest good and cause the least harm. A wise and spiritually mature person can help you sort out the specifics of your particular situation.

5. FACE THE CONSEQUENCES

If you have confessed your sins and repented, know that God has forgiven you. Jesus has traded places with you and has taken your punishment. You do not have to punish yourself for what you have done. He loves you! Having set things right with God brings a deep peace and a new hope. Now he wants to guide you and support you as you make things right with people. For if we have harmed people there will be consequences, even when we've been forgiven by God. When David succumbed to his lust for Bathsheba and committed adultery, he tried to cover it up by murdering her husband. Amazingly God was willing to forgive him, but there were still consequences.

- And Nathan said to David, "The Lord has put away your sin, you shall not die. Nevertheless, because by this deed you have utterly scorned the Lord, the child that is born to you shall die." 2nd Sam 12. 13-14

You need to consider three areas of consequences that you may have to face.

A) *Making Restitution*

Besides admitting what you've done and apologizing for it, you may need to make some kind of restitution. The Biblical idea of restitution is to give back to those you have taken from. This giving back needs to be generous and not half-hearted. It is supposed to come at a significant cost to you.

- He shall confess his sin which he has committed; and he shall make full restitution for his wrong, adding a fifth to it. Num 5.7
- And Zacchaeus stood and said to the Lord, "Behold Lord, the half of my goods I give to the poor; and if I have defrauded anyone of anything, I restore it fourfold." Lk 19.8

Ask God if there is something he would like you to do to improve the life of someone you've harmed. Financial restitution may be in order.

B) *Legal Consequences*

Some behaviours associated with sexual addiction have legal consequences. All level 3, and some level 2 behaviours are considered breaches of Canada's penal code. The Bible is clear regarding the relationship God's people are to have with the laws of the land.

- Let every person be subject to the governing authorities. For there is no authority except from God, and those that exist have been instituted by God. Rom 13.1
- Be subject, for the Lord's sake, to every human institution. 1st Pet 2.13

Admitting the harm you have done, may result in people wanting to press charges against you. This is their right. Victims may wish to seek regress for the harm you have caused them to assist them in their own healing process. Whatever the potential personal loss, (loss of job, reputation, etc.) you need to face up to the legal consequences of your actions. God will want you to admit your guilt and fully accept whatever penalties are imposed. It is wise to speak to a competent lawyer so that you properly understand the charges against you.

C) Social Consequences

Jesus Christ sees through the window of our minds and judges us according to what he sees there.

- Before him no creature is hidden, but all are open and laid bare before him with whom we have to do. Heb 4.13

Because of his special vantage point Jesus sees that we are all sinners, and all need redeeming. In the gospel of John a woman was caught in adultery and Jesus invited people to stone her. There was however one condition, they had to be without sin themselves.

- Let him who is without sin among you be the first to throw a stone at her. Jn 8.7

Thankfully the people on that day realized they were not worthy to condemn her.

- Jesus looked up and said to her, "Woman where are they, has no one condemned you?" She said, "No one Lord."

When you are a sex addict coming out into the light, you are in the same position as this woman. You are she standing ashamed and humiliated before a crowd of your own contemporaries, waiting to be stoned. There are two kinds of people in the crowd. Those who know they are sinners like you, and those who believe they are better than you. Be assured that your confession will bring out the best and worst in your circle. You know that there are some who are going to be picking up stones. This may result in serious social consequences for you. Depending on your past behaviour some or all of your family and friends may not forgive you. They may no longer accept you or want anything to do with you. You will have to accept this loss as a consequence of your actions. You will need to respect their decision. You may have to build a new social network made up of a humbler kind of people.

Put yourself in your victim's shoes

Step 11: Develop Discipline

Wildfires

Normally when we think about wildfires we think only about the damage and devastation they cause. They consume the forest, kill wildlife, destroy property, fill the sky with smoke contributing to green house gasses, and take human life. Only occasionally do we hear about the benefits of forest fires yet naturally occurring fires have always been an important and necessary part of the forest cycle. Fire removes dead and decaying plant matter on the forest floor. This actually ensures that future fires will be less destructive. Fire removes pests and disease thereby improving the health of the surviving trees. Fire thins out the forest so that more light can penetrate the forest floor. This enables the growth of grasses, herbs, and berry bushes providing a mixed forest which is more beneficial to animals. Fire releases nutrients trapped in the trees and returns them to the soil in the form of ash. This renews the forest as new seedlings thrive in the improved soil. In the same way struggling with a sexual addiction is not without it's benefits. Paradoxically your addiction

"In this you rejoice, though now for a little while you may have to suffer various trials, so that the genuineness of your faith, more precious than gold which though perishable is tested by fire."

—1st Pet 1.6-7

can make you a new person just like the wildfire makes a new forest. It is taking on sin and defeating it that enables new spiritual growth. This is how our inner spiritual man becomes stronger than our outer fleshy man; through struggling with fire. Without struggle we can never become strong. There is no other way to become spiritually mature. Accept your out of control behaviour as an opportunity to learn self-control, for this is God's plan for you. Fire has always been the great purifier.

Let Go of Laziness

Self-discipline is the ability to make yourself do something that you don't feel like doing. Everyone suffering from an addiction has weakness in the area of self-discipline. Their willpower has broken down. They may have the will, but not the power. This leaves them vulnerable to temptation.

- A man without self control is like a city broken and left without walls. Pr 25.28

Contrary to what the world currently believes, the Bible does not view addiction as an illness. The Bible sees all addiction as lack of self-control. We simply have made poor choices for which God holds us accountable.

- Do not get drunk with wine for that is debauchery. Eph 5.18
- Whose end is destruction, whose god is their belly, {Their appetites} and whose glory is in their shame - who set their minds on earthly things. Phil 3.19
- So kill (deprive of power) the evil desire lurking in your members: sexual vice, impurity, sensual appetites, unholy desires, and all greed and covetousness which is idolatry. Col 3.5

If God holds us accountable for our addictions then there is no excuse for them. The truth is that addictions are decisions. Life is packed with difficulties we all face: pain, loss, loneliness, stress, discouragement, rejection and a long list of troubles. When we are confronted by difficulty we have a choice as to how we deal with it. We can either turn to God who will show us a healthy way through, or we can turn to our flesh for a quick fix. Addiction really is the result of a character flaw. It develops when we choose the easy way out of difficulty. We are too lazy to do the work that God's holy way requires.

When an addict is ready to change he must return to the crossroads. He must face difficulty anew, but learn how to make healthier choices in it. This is the crucible where self discipline can be learned. God won't make things suddenly easier. He knows difficulty is a necessary ingredient in the reformation of character.

- Suffering produces endurance, endurance produces character, character produces hope. Rom 5.3-4

This is God's recipe and it bears no resemblance to the flesh's easy way out. The flesh wants to take you out of your need and pain; it offers fast, but temporary solutions. God wants you to face your pain, and gradually work through it with him. There are four ingredients to God's recipe for building character strength.

1) SUFFERING

Developing a strong character is no different from developing a strong body, both require suffering. Any athlete in training pushes themselves to the point of discomfort. Weightlifters increase resistance and runners increase distance. They purposefully make things difficult for their bodies so they can build strength and endurance. If only we were so disciplined about building our character.

- Train yourself in godliness; for while bodily training is of some value, godliness is of value in every way. 1st Tim 4.8

Begin by looking differently at the things in your life that are causing you difficulty. Stop just running away and trying to escape from your problems. Stand in the crossroad for a little while and have a look. Maybe the difficulties are there for a reason. Maybe they are the very things you need to help you grow stronger. Maybe God has intentionally allowed suffering to come into your life. Maybe your problem is actually a gift to help you discover the ways of the Spirit.

- Beloved do not be surprised at the fiery ordeal which comes upon you to prove you as though something strange were happening to you. 1st Pet 4.12

- It was good for me that I was afflicted, that I might learn thy statutes. Ps 119.71
- Come let us return to the Lord; for he has torn, that he may heal us. Hos 6.1

My marriage is a mess, I hate my job, I'm in serious debt, I've got health problems, I'm so lonely, I'm depressed. Whichever hardship it is, it is not necessarily your enemy and you don't have to be so afraid of it. Try to accept it and welcome it into your life because it may be your best teacher. Realize that the greatest treasures in life come not from what is easy, but from what is difficult.

- For the moment all discipline feels painful rather than pleasant. Heb 12.11

2) ENDURANCE

In the area of our addiction we are wimps. When faced with difficulty and temptation we just cave in; there is no mental toughness in us. There is only one way to build toughness of will and that is through resistance.

- Let not sin therefore reign in your mortal bodies, to make you obey their passions. Do not yield your members to sin as instruments of wickedness. Rom 6.12-13

When temptation arises, and you know it will, are you just going to let it keep pushing you around? Are you always going to be intimidated by it or is the day here when you start standing up for yourself? If you're ready to start dealing with this bully it is best to have a plan.

a) Anticipate - Know your triggers

When are you most likely to be tempted? Is it when you are anxious and stressed? Is it when you are tired, or when you are around certain people? Is it when you are exposed to certain media? Is it when you are lonely? Think about it and try to recognize your temptation pattern.

b) Reduce - Remove triggers

Are there some changes you could make in your life that would reduce your triggers? Are there people you should not be alone with?

Should you place restrictions on yourself with the internet? Can you do something about your stress level, or the amount of loneliness you feel?

c) *Use diversions* - Give temptation some competition

Sexual temptations are accompanied by strong urges. You can reduce the urges by diverting your attention away from them. Try getting busy with a project that demands your full attention. Hard physical exercise works for many. If you are musical give yourself an hour of intense practice. Go and do something kind for someone. The key is to get yourself doing.

d) *Control your thought life* - Interrupt temptation at the source

Sexual temptation happens in the mind. We don't commit sin unless we sin first in our minds. When you learn to exercise control over what you're thinking, you will be far more able to control your actions. We can learn to diminish our impure thoughts by training our minds to be occupied with more positive things.

e) *Engage with people* - You don't have to face the bully alone

Seek out supportive healthy friends that you can do things with. It may be someone to talk to about your struggle or just good people to be around. Temptation and sin tend to be isolating forces because of the guilt and shame associated with them. Just being around loving and accepting people is strengthening to the spirit.

3) CHARACTER

The suggestions above will help you ameliorate temptations, but they will not eliminate them. You will still have to resist because resistance is required for character building. When we are weak and have no character strength we give away our power to the enemies of our spirit. We are no longer in charge of our lives because we have given away the control of them. Who is it anyway that wants so badly to control us, who is my enemy?

A) *Satan* - You may have difficulty accepting it, but if you are enslaved to sin you are to some degree, under satan's power. The Bible is clear in its warning that there are powers of darkness opposed to us. This means that in the spiritual realm there are beings that have a personal vendetta against you and want to harm you.

- Your adversary the devil prowls around like a roaring lion, seeking someone to devour. 1st Per 5.8

Don't be surprised that you can't plainly see their activities. They always use subterfuge and trickery in an attempt to conceal their operations.

- And no wonder, for even satan disguises himself as an angel of light. 2nd Cor 11.14

One of their main weapons they will use against you is temptation.

- For this reason, when I could bear it no longer, I sent that I might know your faith, for fear that somehow the tempter had tempted you and that our labour would be in vain. 1st Thess 3.5

Ask God to reveal to you the role that the devil has in your temptation cycle. Ask him to show you your addiction as it is seen in the spiritual realm. This can be a startling discovery and a tremendous help in recovery, because once the devil has been exposed and resisted he retreats.

- Resist the devil and he will flee from you. Jam 4.7

B) Sin - Sin is a bragging bully strutting around the playground muttering threats. It wants you to believe that you can't beat it, and to not bother even trying. It wants you to be convinced that you are destined to be dominated by it. This is utter nonsense. Remember that our definition of sin is doing what we know displeases God. Displeasing God is a choice we make voluntarily. The only power sin has over us is what we willingly give it. Remember that the very reason Jesus died was to free you from bondage to sin and give you back the power to choose.

- For sin will have no dominion over you. Rom 6.14
- But now that you have been set free from sin and have become slaves of God, the return you get is sanctification and its end, eternal life. Rom 5.22
- For freedom Christ has set us free; stand fast therefore, and do not submit again to a yoke of slavery. Gal 5.1

We are meant to live an impossible life, a life of purity and holiness no longer under the tyranny of sin. But what so many of us don't grasp is that we can't accomplish this in the flesh.

Taking on sin in your own strength is a battle you cannot win.

- For the mind that is set on the flesh is hostile to God; it does not submit to God's law, indeed it cannot; Rom 8.7

It is only by: drawing near to God, submitting your whole life to him, walking in the Spirit, and being filled with his word, that you can realize freedom from sin.

- So then brethren, we are debtors, not to the flesh, to live according to the flesh - for if you live according to the flesh you will die, but if by the Spirit you put to death the deeds of the body you will live. Rom 8.12-13

C) Self - When we have run off the devil, and faced down sin, we still have the self to contend with. Our fallen and self-centered ego wants to rule our lives. It doesn't want us to live for Jesus, it is opposed to putting his will first. It relentlessly strives for our obedience and is never satisfied until we bow down to it. The self is so strong in us and so permeating all our thinking that there is only one way to be free of its rule; it has to die.

- If any man would come after me, let him deny his self and take up his cross and follow me. For whoever would save his life will lose it, and whoever loses his life for my sake will find it. Mt 16.24-25

- Whoever finds his {lower} life will lose his {higher} life, and whoever loses his {lower} life on my account, will find it {the higher life}. Mt 10.39

This is the ultimate freedom; freedom from self, but in order to achieve it we must die with Christ. We must let go completely of our whole life with all our plans, ambitions, and desires. We must give it all up and trade our life for his so that we exist now only for God's plans, ambitions, and desires.

- We know that the old self was crucified with him so that the sinful body might be destroyed, and we might no longer be enslaved to sin. Rom 6. 6

- I have been crucified with Christ; it is no longer I who live, but Christ who lives in me. Gal 2.20

- And he died for all, that those who live might no longer live for themselves, but for him who for their sake died. 2 Cor 5.15

If you are sick and tired of your self this is the way to be rid of it. Bring it to God and lay it at his feet, tell him that you are done living for your self.

Enemies without and enemies within are a necessary part of this Christian life. They are there for a reason. Without enemies there is no victory over enemies. Without struggle there is no development of strength. If you meet someone with strong character and spiritual power how do you think this was achieved? Our struggle with satan, sin, and self, is the very ground where our character is proven. This is where we take back our self control, vanquish our foes, and discover our strength and dignity through Christ.

- Blessed is the man who endures trial, for when he has stood the test he will receive the crown of life which God has promised to those that love him. Jam 1.12
- For God has not given us a spirit of timidity, but of power, and of love, and of self-control. 2nd Tim 1.7

4) HOPE

Moral fitness and freedom from sexual addiction is not a gift, it is something you earn. Just like physical fitness it is not instant, but comes gradually through persistence. And just like getting in better shape physically, you can expect to have setbacks and delays. It is best to be aware of this from the start so that when you fall you don't lose the precious treasure that God has planted in your heart - hope. Hope is the ability to see how things can be different. It is the belief in possibility. This noble quality is growing inside you but you do have enemies that will try to rob you of it. They will use your stumbles and falls to accuse you and try to convince that it is impossible for you to change.

- Then he showed me Joshua the high priest standing before the angel of the Lord, and Satan standing at his right hand to accuse him... Now Joshua was standing before the angel clothed with filthy garments Zech 3. 1-4

If satan can get you to lose hope he's got you where he wants you.

- Hope deferred makes the heart sick. Pr 13.12

So how can you prepare yourself for setbacks and not get discouraged by them?

Jeremiah the prophet struggled with deep disappointment and discouragement.

- My soul is bereft of peace, I have forgotten what happiness is; so I say gone is my glory and my expectation from the Lord. Lam 3.17-18

He had a method that he used to help him keep going and to not give up hope.

- But this I call to mind and therefore I have hope. Lam 3.21

Jeremiah understood that discouragement happens in the mind. It comes from thinking discouraging thoughts so he deliberately would fill his mind with encouraging and hopeful thoughts. Below is a list of these thoughts taken directly from his own positive self talk found in Lamentations chapter three.

JEREMIAH'S LIST

The steadfast love of the Lord never ceases

His mercies never come to an end

His mercies are new every morning

God's faithfulness is great

The Lord is my portion, says my soul, therefore I will hope in him

The Lord is good to those who wait for him

The Lord is good to those that seek him

The Lord will not cast off forever

Though he cause grief, he will have compassion

He does not willingly afflict or grieve the sons of men

When we feel discouraged, and the devil is trying to accuse us and steal our hope, we don't have to just sit there and take it whimpering. We can stand up to discouragement and stop the negative self talk. Be prepared for accusation beforehand with your own Jeremiah list. Choose scriptures about God's love for you that encourage you. Do what all great saints of God have learned to do; stand upon the promises of God.

- The promises of the Lord are promises that are pure, silver refined in a furnace on the ground, purified seven times. Ps 12.6

- By which he has granted to us his precious and very great promises, that through these you may escape from the corruption that is in the world because of passion and become partakers of the divine nature. 2nd Pet. 1.4

MY JEREMIAH LIST

_____

_____

_____

_____

_____

_____

_____

_____

_____

_____

_____

_____

_____

_____

_____

_____

_____

_____

Jesus knows already that you are going to stumble. He understands that winning back self-discipline takes time. He knows all about gradual growth. In fact he knows that if change comes too quickly, it doesn't last.

- Other seeds fell on rocky ground, where they had not much soil, and immediately they sprang up, since they had no depth of soil, but when the sun rose they were scorched; and since they had no root they withered away. Mt 13 5-6

His main concern is that when you get knocked down that you aren't crushed under a load of accusation and discouragement. He wants you to get up, brush yourself off and get back in the fight. Stubbornly refuse to give up your hope.

- For a righteous man falls seven times and rises again. Pr 24.16

"The way is hard that leads to life." Mt 7.14

NOTES

_____

_____

_____

_____

_____

_____

_____

_____

_____

_____

_____

Step 12: Control Your Mind

Hotspots

After a wildfire has finally been brought under control the job of fire-fighting is not yet complete. There remains a mopping up stage that can take several weeks as crews search the burnt ground for hotspots. These are small localized under-ground fires that are still smouldering although no flame can be seen. Fire crews spread out walking in a systematic grid pattern to be sure every meter of ground is inspected. When they find any area that is smoking or hot to the touch, they douse it with water and use shovels and axes to turn the ground over. They dig up any smoking roots or stumps and then douse the area with water a second time. Rooting up stumps and hauling heavy hose through the debris is back breaking work, but the crews will not move out of an area until all ash is cold to the touch and they are confident the fire will not come back to life.

"As I mused, the fire burned."

— Ps 39.3

In the same way when we have managed to bring our behaviour back under control the job is not yet over. To be sure that our problem doesn't just resurface a few weeks or months down the road we must get below the surface. We must dig deep and extinguish the fire in our minds to be sure it is really out. As long as we are still thinking or imagining sin, we are not yet free from it.

Let Go Of Impurity

The Holy Spirit's aim is to make us like Jesus Christ and this should be the aim of every Christian.

- And we all with unveiled face, beholding the glory of the Lord, are being changed into his likeness from one degree of glory to another; for this comes from the Lord who is the Spirit. 2nd Cor 3.18

Jesus not only wants to share his love with us but all aspects of himself, including his holiness and righteousness. Holiness is an inner purity that resides in the heart and mind. A pure mind is the key to pure behaviour.

- So, every sound tree bears good fruit, but the bad tree bears evil fruit. A sound tree cannot bear evil fruit, nor can a bad tree bear good fruit. Mt 7.17-18

Jesus is looking for a purity that is not only refraining from outer sin, but also refraining from inner sin. He understands human nature. He knows that as long as we have evil thoughts our hearts have not really changed; we are still being ruled by the flesh. We won't be truly free of sexual addiction until our minds are.

- But I say that everyone who looks at a woman lustfully has already committed adultery with her in his heart. Mt 5.28

God does not only judge us by our behaviour, but also by what he observes in our hearts and minds. He peers inside us to see who we really are.

- I, the Lord, search the mind and try the heart, and give to every man according to his ways, according to the fruit of his doings. Jer 17.10

Jesus taught that his disciples are held to a very high standard, a standard that goes beyond superficial morality to genuine inner purity.

- For I tell you, unless your righteousness exceeds that of the scribes and Pharisees, you will never enter the kingdom of heaven. Mt 5.20

As has already been pointed out in this course, this kind of inner beauty cannot be achieved by mere human effort. It is meant to be accomplished by surrendering ourselves to the working of the Holy Spirit as he, degree by degree sanctifies us. This process is not formulaic but varies with each individual. It is dependent on a close relationship with God as he leads us into purity and we obediently follow.

- Work out your own salvation with fear and trembling for God is at work in you both to will and to work for his good pleasure. Phil 2.12-13

As the Holy Spirit is at work in us there are some things we can do to be working on our own salvation. Below are a list of covenants you can make with yourself that will help you gain control of your thought life. Don't attempt them all at once, but work through them slowly and steadily. Pray the Spirit to enable you.

1) A COVENANT WITH YOUR EYES

Looking lustfully at a woman is displeasing to God. It is connected to our thought life because we are imagining the woman naked. Job understood that no man of God who is living to please the Lord can entertain such thoughts.

- I have made a covenant with my eyes; how then could I look upon a virgin? What would be my portion from God above, and my heritage from the almighty on high? Job 31.1-2

You too can make a covenant with your eyes. Begin with getting through one day without looking at women lustfully. When you can do that, try two days and so on. For some men a simple aversion technique has proven helpful. Try wearing a heavy elastic band around your wrist and discreetly giving yourself a snap when your eyes stray. With the Spirit's help and some determination, you can retrain yourself to start seeing women as Jesus does and no longer as objects of desire.

2) A COVENANT WITH MEDIA

We live in a culture where entertainment is a priority. Embedded in so much entertainment are images and messages that are carnal. It's not until we start to clean up our minds that we even realize all the filth that has accumulated there. When we sincerely give our lives to Jesus Christ we need to understand that we hand over our minds to him too.

- Do you not know that your body is a temple of the Holy Spirit within you, which you have from God? You are not your own; you were bought with a price. So glorify God in your body. 1st Cor 6.19-20.
- I appeal therefore, brethren, and beg of you in view of {all} the mercies of God, to make a decisive dedication of your bodies {presenting all your members and faculties} as a living sacrifice. Rom 12.1

God asks us to make an offering of all our faculties including our minds. Can we accept this idea that our mind is no longer ours but belongs to Jesus? As we start to take a closer look at what we expose our minds to we begin to question ourselves; is this something Jesus is comfortable watching or listening to? Take stock of all your contacts with worldly media: television shows, music, video games, movies, magazines and books, internet sites, etc. Make a covenant with yourself that you will only permit exposure to what is good for your spirit. Decide that you will no longer participate in what draws your flesh. Work through your list one area at a time until you have reformed all your media contacts to ones Jesus approves of. Be a nonconformist and no longer allow the current entertainment culture to mold your mind.

- Do not be conformed to this world, but be transformed by the renewal of your mind. Rom 12.2

3) A COVENANT WITH YOUR MIND

Our mind is an amazing gift capable of wonderful creativity and intelligence. Unfortunately it is also severely corrupted and interested in evil.

- The Lord saw that the wickedness of man was great in the earth, and that every imagination of the thoughts of his heart was only evil continually. Gen 6.5

We are called to use our gifts for good and not for evil and this includes our minds.

- Do not yield your members to sin as instruments of wickedness, but yield yourselves to God as men who have been brought from death to life, and your members to God as instruments of righteousness. Rom 6.13

The Bible teaches that through the Spirit we are capable of bringing our thoughts into obedience to Jesus.

- Casting down imaginations and every high thing that exalts itself against the knowledge of God, and bringing into captivity every thought to the obedience of Christ. 2nd Cor 10.5

The truth is that we can control what our minds are doing and are thus responsible for our thought life. Indeed what occupies our minds is a true reflection of who we really are.

- As in water face answers to face, so the mind of man reflects the man. Pr 27.19
- For as he thinks in his heart, so is he. Pr 23.7

Getting control over your thought life is a dual process. The first step is making a covenant with yourself that you are not going to allow your imagination to serve sin anymore. This is a form of putting off your old nature.

- Put off your old nature which belongs to your former manner of life and is corrupt through deceitful lusts. Eph 4.22

However, it will not be enough for you to just try to stop sinful thoughts. The mind abhors a vacuum; it needs to be occupied with something. So the second step is to give your mind better things to be occupied with. This is how you can put on the new nature. When our thoughts become like Jesus' thoughts, then we will become like Jesus.

- Be renewed in the spirit of your minds, and put on the new nature, created after the likeness of God in true holiness and righteousness. Eph 4.24

It all has to do with developing a new mind set. If you are still in the flesh and living for yourself, your thoughts will be occupied with things of the flesh. If you are walking in the Spirit your thoughts will be focused on spiritual things.

- For those who live according to the flesh set their mind on the things of the flesh, but those who live according to the Spirit set their mind on the things of the Spirit. Rom 8.5
- Set your minds on things that are above and not on things that are on earth. Col 3.2

103

Developing a spiritual mindset is simply occupying your mind with things that are not earthly. Below are just a few samples of what beautiful minds are busy with.

A New Mind Set

A) Prayer - Pray at all times in the Spirit with all prayer and supplication. Eph 6.18

B) Gratitude - Pray constantly, give thanks in all circumstances. 1st Thess 5.18

C) Pondering the Positive - Finally brethren whatever is true, whatever is honourable, whatever is just, whatever is pure, whatever is lovely, whatever is gracious, if there is any excellence, if there is anything worthy of praise, think about these things. Phil 3.8

D) Planning Good - Those who devise good meet loyalty and faithfulness. Pr 14.22

E) Learning - Apply your mind to instruction and your ear to words of knowledge. Pr 23.12

F) Meditating on Scripture - I have more understanding than all my teachers for thy testimonies are my meditation. Ps 119.99

G) Creativity - I have filled him (Bezalel) with the Spirit of God, with ability and intelligence, with knowledge and all craftsmanship, to devise artistic designs. Ex 31.3

H) Empathy for the Suffering - Remember those in prison as though in prison with them; and those who are ill treated, since you also are in the body. Heb 13.3

Becoming spiritually minded may seem strange at first. It certainly is a whole new way of perceiving life but you will find it a powerful tool when facing temptation. When your thoughts start to stray take control of them. Give your mind something else to do. Pray, sing, praise, create, write, memorize scripture, learn something mentally challenging. Rather than multi-tasking, learn to uni-task and become deliberately focused and immersed in healthy and directed mental activity.

To become like Jesus we must learn to think like Jesus.

Meditation verses: Rev 2.6, Pr 6. 16-19, Pr 8.13, Eccl 3.11, Rom 8.7, Rev 3.4, Jude 22-23, Rev 16.15, Zech 3.1-5

NOTES

_____

_____

_____

_____

_____

_____

_____

_____

_____

_____

_____

_____

Sexual Addiction Survey

never	occasionally	regularly	frequently	constantly
0	1	2	3	4

1.	View pornography	
2.	Have impure thought life	
3.	Look at women lustfully	
4.	Am secretive about my addiction	
5.	Am reluctant to seek out help	
6.	Feel distant from God	
7.	Bible seems dry and lifeless	
8.	Have difficulty with self-control	
9.	Have inappropriate relationships (flirtatious ones included)	
10.	Think holiness is impossible	
11.	Have tendency to be self-absorbed	
12.	Avoid considering how my problem affects others	
13.	Share the notion that Christians have nothing to fear from God	
14.	Make excuses to minimize seriousness of my problem	
15.	Procrastinating on genuine repentance	
16.	Resist submitting all areas of life to Jesus	
17.	Unwilling to take responsibility for changing my life	

Total: _____

ADDICTION SCORE

Imminent danger........57-68	*CONFLAGRATION*
Out of control..............46-57	*CROWN FIRE*
Losing control.............34-46	*VIGOROUS SURFACE FIRE*
Habitual 23-34	*RUNNING SURFACE FIRE*
Troublesome...............12-23	*LOW VIGOUR SURFACE FIRE*
Mild and infrequent....0-12	*SMOULDERING GROUND FIRE*